Achieving Greatness with God

Achieving Greatness with God

How Your Efforts
+
God's Power
=
Ultimate Success

Jarrod Bentley

Published by Leon Street Publishing

Certain names and identifying characteristics mentioned in this book have been changed.

ISBN: 978-0-9834682-0-2

Printed in the United States of America

www.greatnesswithgod.com

www.jarrodbentley.com

CONTENTS

Introduction

I remember the phone call that changed my life. I was finishing my day at work when a receptionist from my doctor's office called and nonchalantly announced, "Mr. Bentley, your tests results are in, and you have a tumor behind your right eye that needs to be removed immediately. I've scheduled an appointment with a specialist tomorrow, and he will advise you about your surgical options." She then gave me the details of where I was to go the next day and abruptly hung up.

Talk about a surreal experience! I had only recently complained to my doctor about experiencing some mild headaches, and now I was being told that I needed immediate surgery to remove a tumor. One moment I was excited to be done with work. The next, I was wondering if I was going to die.

When I met with the specialist the next day, I was advised that the shape of the tumor looked troubling and it needed to be removed as quickly as possible. I was also told that, although the surgery to do this was fairly routine, because of the location of this tumor, there were significant risks, including that of permanent eye damage and even blindness. Despite these risks, the specialist reinforced how important it was to remove the tumor, and to do it as quickly as possible. Taking this advice, I scheduled a surgery for a couple weeks out. In the meantime, however, I figured it was in my best interest to get a second opinion.

A few days later, I visited a new specialist, and sure enough,

I got a completely different diagnosis. This new specialist told me that the shape of the tumor looked fine and having it removed probably wasn't necessary. He recommended against surgery and instead suggested I wait to see how things progressed. Pardon the pun, but he wanted me to keep an eye on things. As an added precaution, he also suggested that I undergo a few extra tests to make sure everything else in my body was okay. I agreed to do this and left his office feeling like everything was going to be fine.

Per the new specialist's instructions, I underwent a full body scan, and although I went into this test feeling pretty good, I certainly didn't come out that way. To my total disbelief, this new scan revealed a tumor in my bladder. I couldn't believe it! First the tumor behind my eye and now a tumor in my bladder. What was going on with my body?

Now, before I continue with what happened, allow me to share a little background about who I am, and why I have written this book. Ever since I can remember, the subject of prayer has totally fascinated me. The very idea that God can bless us with the things we ask for, is such a powerful concept that it warrants, rather demands, further investigation.

If accomplishing your goals and realizing your dreams is made easier when you pray, doesn't it make sense to learn everything you can about prayer? Of course it does. And aren't you like everybody else? In most situations, aren't you looking for the proverbial "leg up?" Well, here it is. Grab hold because I guarantee that prayer is the ticket to a better life.

Just think about it. What would it be like if you were able to achieve all of your goals and dreams? How much better would your relationships be? How much happier would you be? What amazing things would you be doing right now if all the limitations and barriers to success were removed? Well, that's what can happen when you incorporate prayer more into your life.

But what makes me such an expert on the subject? After all,

it's not like I'm a preacher or a minister. So why should you listen to me talk about prayer?

Well, two reasons.

First, I have been privileged to experience countless examples of where God has answered my prayers, and done so in some truly remarkable ways. Beginning as a child, where I learned valuable insights into how prayer could help me achieve the things I most wanted. As a young man, where my prayers led me to volunteer as a Christian missionary in the Australian Outback. Here my faith in Jesus and the power of prayer were strengthened beyond description and I witnessed how prayer can truly bring about miracles. Now as a husband and father, God continues to answer my prayers and bless my family in a truly awe-inspiring manner.

After having had so many prayer related experiences, many of which I will share with you in this book, I know that prayer works. It will not only bring us closer to God, but also it can absolutely help us more readily achieve our goals. Armed with this knowledge I feel duty bound to share it with others.

Second, I truly believe that I have been called to share my thoughts on prayer with others. In fact, for the better part of ten years I have had an overwhelming feeling to write this book, and as much as I have tried to ignore this feeling, it has persisted. It has gnawed at my very soul to the point where I find myself compelled to put pen to paper and write about my insights.

In complete sincerity, putting this book together has been a monumental undertaking. I have never felt more inadequate or overwhelmed in my life. I am neither a writer, nor a religious scholar. I'm just an ordinary person trying my best to encourage others to pray. I fully appreciate that my knowledge is far from complete and that I make mistakes. With that in mind, I ask that as you read this book to overlook my shortcomings and know that my motives are pure. I simply want you to catch a glimpse of how completely magnificent your life can be as you develop a better relationship with God through prayer.

In doing the research to write this book, I have tried to learn as much as I possibly could about prayer. I have read dozens of prayer books, interviewed hundreds of prayerful people, immersed myself in Scripture, and most important, I have spent countless hours on my knees, imploring God for a greater understanding of how prayer actually works. Now, although I still have so very much to learn, I feel what I have learned is so valuable that's it worth repeating. Plus, I've made some really exciting discoveries about how your prayers can more readily help you achieve all of your goals and dreams that I can't wait to share.

For now though, let me get back to discussing the situation with my health. As you might imagine, as I was trying to figure out what was going on with my body, I said my fair share of prayers asking God to bless me. However, one prayer in particular stands out. One night, in the midst of this turmoil, I was asking God to give me the comfort I was looking for and the assurance that everything was going to be okay. And that's when it happened.

While I was pleading with God to heal me, I had one of the most special prayer experiences of my life. As I was kneeling down beside my bed, pouring my heart out to God, I felt a burning within my chest and throughout my body that was so completely overwhelming that it felt like God Himself was wrapping me in His arms. This was one of the most exquisite, beautiful, and reassuring feelings that I had ever felt, and was accompanied by a sense of peace and love that was just as remarkable. This experience lasted for several minutes and although I had received answers to my prayers before, I had never felt anything as magnificent as this.

Without question, I knew what I was feeling was from God and He was clearly telling me that, not only did He exist, but also that I didn't need to worry about what was going to happen. So, from that moment on, I placed my complete trust in God with the understanding that He knew my situation and would take care of me. Now, don't get me wrong. I didn't know exactly how everything was going to work out. I just knew that it would.

A few days later, I went in to have the tumor in my bladder examined with a little more scrutiny and that's when something remarkable happened. The doctor performing these new tests couldn't find this tumor. He looked again and again, but, sure enough, it wasn't there. It had somehow disappeared. Neither my doctor nor I could believe it. My initial body scans show the definite presence of a mass inside my bladder, but, after saying the prayer I mentioned previously and feeling God's love and assurance the way I did, the tumor in my bladder was gone. It had miraculously vanished.

As for the tumor behind my eye, it's been nearly ten years since I first discovered it. To date, it hasn't grown, and everything seems fine. And while I don't think about it all that often, I certainly think about the overall experience. It really did change my life and gave me a new perspective on how to look at things, but not in the way you might think.

You see, having God intervene in my life in such a miraculous way made me question why I wasn't calling on Him more. If He could heal me, then why couldn't He help me do other things?

And then it became crystal clear.

I realized that my prayers could open the very windows of heaven and give me access to God's power in every area of my life, no matter what that was. Whether I needed help with my job, my family, my health- or whatever else, God could help. But more than just giving me a little bit of help, because God can do anything, He could give me unlimited help.

I wish that I could properly describe how much of an epiphany this was to me. It was one of those moments where everything clicked and I had a perfect understanding that I truly could achieve greatness with God's help. And that's when I began this amazing journey to uncover the secrets to prayer.

Now, having discovered so many incredible insights, I feel obligated to share it with you. I want to help you more fully appreciate how much God loves you and how prayer can help you develop a more perfect relationship with Him. Most of all, I want you to know that having a relationship with God like this will undoubtedly make every aspect of your life better!

I invite you to come on this wonderful journey with me. I know that, as you do, you will gain valuable, life-changing insight into how God can bless your life with an overwhelming degree of prosperity, abundance, and happiness. I know this because it has happened for me, and it can happen for you, too!

So are you ready to begin? Then let's get started.

Chapter One

With God, You can Have it All

For all things are possible with God.

Mark 10:27

I freely admit that I want more out of life. A lot more. I want to be a better husband as well as a better father. I want to live a long, productive, healthy life. I want to be more successful and make more money. I want to vacation more, play more, and spend more time with my family. I want to exercise more, entertain more, laugh more, love more... Simply put, I want more. And you know what? You should want more too!

Sadly though, many of us get only a small portion of the things we really want. We barely catch a glimpse of what's possible and end up either settling on what we have, or even worse, giving up entirely. But the truth is it doesn't have to be that way. You can achieve all of your goals and live all of your dreams, and it can be a lot easier than you might think. That's because you have direct access to someone who is all-powerful, who loves you more than you can possibly comprehend, and who wants to help you achieve your goals.

Who is this someone? It's God. Your very loving, very powerful, Father in Heaven. So whether your heart's desire is spiritual, physical, emotional, or even financial, with God's help you can accomplish anything. And I mean anything.

God created the world and everything in it. He is certainly capable of intervening in your life to help you accomplish your goals.

The best way to access God's help is through the magnificent process of prayer. Just consider what Jesus revealed to His disciples about what was possible with prayer.

> *And Jesus answered them…"But even if you say to this mountain, 'Be taken up and thrown into the sea,' it will happen.*
>
> *And whatever you ask in prayer, you will receive, if you have faith."*
>
> (Matt 21:21–22)

Think about this Scripture in relation to the things you're looking to achieve. Your goals might seem difficult, or even impossible, but don't worry. Simply remember what God is capable of. With His infinite power, He created the world and everything in it. He is certainly capable of intervening in your life to help you accomplish your goals, no matter what they might be. The simple truth is that although something might seem impossible to you, it isn't for God. As Jesus declares, prayer is so powerful that, with it, not only do you have the ability to move mountains, but you also have the ability to do anything else. The only prerequisite is that you have faith. Faith in the belief that God can answer your prayers, as well as faith in Jesus Christ.

Best of all, provided you have the faith that Jesus mentions, the amazing blessings of prayer are available to everyone. It simply doesn't matter what race you are, how old you are, or how much money you have. Prayer can bind every single person in the world with God and to each other, and without question, it is one of the most powerful tools that God has blessed us with.

The bottom line is that with prayer you can receive blessings from God that you otherwise wouldn't, and these blessings can be so remarkable that you will want them. But, you must know how to pray the right way, and you must understand how prayer works. And that's exactly what this book will teach.

God Can Do Anything

Consider this. A recent Harris Poll, "The Religious and Other Beliefs of Americans," has revealed that 90 percent of the United States' population believes in God. Now while this is certainly good news, I would suggest that many of these believers actually underestimate the power and generosity of the God they claim to believe in.

What a shame! To have enough faith to believe in God but not enough to believe that He can bless you with the things you most want. Allow me to share a personal story that helps highlight this point.

Many years ago, I overheard a conversation at church where a group of people were debating on how to best pray for the health of a seriously ill friend. While some in the group suggested that the congregation should ask God to completely heal this person, others suggested that such prayers weren't appropriate and everyone should prepare for the inevitable.

Now while this person's outlook was dire, it certainly didn't warrant these church-going "people of faith" to underestimate God's power or willingness to help. As it happens, this seriously ill friend defied the odds and, through the blessings of God, made a full recovery.

The point here is that because God can do anything, He can answer any prayer. Better yet, because He loves you so much, He is more than willing to help you. But how do you actually garner His help and receive His blessings? Well, that's what I'm here to answer, but, before I do, let me be perfectly clear on something.

Prayer is not a substitute for hard work, and God is not some kind of spiritual Santa Claus looking to grant your every wish. That's not how prayer works. Instead, prayer is a tool that can help you develop a more perfect relationship with God, and this relationship can be leveraged to bless your life in ways that otherwise wouldn't happen. But, receiving these blessings involves following certain steps, and unless you're familiar with these steps and follow them precisely, it's unlikely that God will bless you with everything you're looking for.

The bottom line is there are guidelines to receiving blessings from God, and throughout this book, I will reveal these guidelines to you. Then, as you come to know what these are, and do your best to live by them, you will be eligible for God to more fully bless your life. Plus, keep in mind that, when God does bless you, He can do so in a completely overwhelming and abundant manner.

God Did the Rest

I wanted more out of life than just going to work every day. I wanted to play with my kids more and be with my wife more. Unfortunately, my job was so time-consuming that I felt like I wasn't being the husband and father I wanted to be. That I knew I could be. I really wanted things to be different, and I began to ask God for help. I mostly asked that He would help me find a new job that wouldn't require me to be away from home so much.

It wasn't long afterwards that, completely unexpectedly, an old friend called me about a job opening at his company. He said that he felt like he had to call me about this position. He thought I'd be perfect for this job and really encouraged me to look into it.

I decided to pursue the opportunity and after many interviews, and many prayers, I eventually landed this job and have been working for this company ever since.

This change was just what I needed. I now have the flexibility to spend more time with my family and I feel like I'm becoming the husband and father I always wanted to be. Interestingly, before I even started to seriously look for a new job, my friend called and told me about the opening at his company. All I did was pray and ask for help. Remarkably, God did the rest!

I am so grateful to have a Heavenly Father who loves me so much, who knows what I'm going through, and is willing to help me. God was aware of my situation, and it turns out that He wanted what I wanted, for me to be happy.

Jim M. - Texas

Calling upon the powers of heaven and having God help you achieve greatness involves following certain steps, and we will go over these steps in great detail. First, however, it's important that you understand four basic concepts that relate to prayer. Once understood, these concepts will enable you to learn the secrets to prayer and more readily unleash the awesome power of God in your life. These four concepts of prayer are:

1. *God Wants You to Be Great.*
2. *You Need to Ask for What You Want.*
3. *There are Rules to Prayer.*
4. *God Wants You to Be Happy.*

1. God Wants You to Be Great

Unfortunately, during the course of my conversations with the hundreds of people who pray (or who think they pray), I have been struck by how many people, though they wholeheartedly believe in God and pray regularly, feel it is forbidden to ask God to bless them with all the desires of their heart. They consider that petitions for wealth and material blessings (and oftentimes even personal happiness) are off-limits. They erroneously think that God doesn't want to bless them with the things they most want. I assure you that nothing could be further from the truth!

Instead, because God loves you so very much, He is eager to bless you. And, like any loving father, as your Heavenly Father, He will go to great lengths to help you accomplish all of your goals and dreams, reach your full potential, and above all, help you be completely and totally happy.

All too often we try to accomplish everything on our own and we fail to recognize that our all-powerful, all-loving God can make our lives a whole lot easier.

Whether you have realized it or not, God has big plans for you, and you should never question what you're capable of achieving with His help. In fact, if you let Him, God can and will improve your life. However, more than just improving your life in a small way, God can improve your life in an enormous way. So frequently, though, we tend to put limitations on what we think God is willing to do for us, and by doing so, we underestimate His ability to intervene in our lives.

Think about that for a moment. God knows everything, He can do anything, and most important, He loves us. Yet we, with our limited knowledge, presuppose to know the extent to which God will bless His children. To me, that just doesn't make sense.

The truth is, that for many of us, God represents a completely untapped power. That's because, all too often, we try to accomplish everything on our own and we fail to recognize that our all-powerful, all-loving God can make our lives a whole lot easier. If we'd just call on Him a little more and invite Him to help us, we'd get a lot more of what we want. Sadly though, we assume God won't bless us and that He doesn't want to reward us with the things we want. While we may acknowledge that He is all-powerful, we simply fail to appreciate His willingness to use His incredible power to bless our lives.

God Can Bless You with So Much More

God does indeed want to bless you and help you achieve your goals, regardless of how lofty or extravagant they might seem. In fact, a Scripture in Matthew highlights this very point. It's where Jesus is talking to a group of people about what God is willing to give. In Matthew 7:9–11, it reads:

> *Or which one of you, if his son asks him for bread, will give him a stone?*
>
> *Or if he asks for a fish, will give him a serpent?*
>
> *If you then, who are evil, know how to give good gifts to your children, how much more will your Father who is in heaven give good things to those who ask him!*

In this passage, Jesus says that if an evil person, which really just refers to someone who's not perfect (in other words you and me), is willing to give his children whatever they ask for, then certainly, God who is perfect, will also give, but even more than expected. The difference, of course, is that when God gives, He can do so without limits.

If you ask God for some bread, He will give you some bread. If you ask for a fish, He'll give you a fish. But more than this, provided your petitions will lead to "gifts that are good," God can bless you with so much more. In fact, if you go about it the right way, God can bless you with anything you want. That's because God doesn't put restrictions on what He's willing to do for His children. We're the ones who typically do that. In the above Scripture, Jesus didn't say, "To those who ask so long as it's not too much." He said, "To those who ask." Period!

A Mother's Plea

There's no other way to say it. My son was born with a big head. Now don't get me wrong. He was still a cute little boy. He just had an abnormally large head. Why do I share this? Well, let me tell you a story about him.

I was out shopping one day when my son, who was two years old at the time, started vomiting all over the floor at the local K-Mart. After apologizing to the shop attendants, I took him to the local doctor and after undergoing some tests, I was told that my son had viral meningitis. An ambulance was called to rush him to the nearest hospital.

While riding to the hospital, I thought of a special school for handicapped children where my mother worked. I remembered how some of these children were severely mentally challenged and how the dreadful meningitis virus had caused their challenges. I also knew that many children who get this virus didn't survive, and I couldn't help but feel completely hopeless.

After a few weeks in the hospital, my son's health deteriorated to the point where the doctors weren't at all optimistic about his chances. In fact, things were so dire that I was told that he probably wouldn't make it through the coming week.

I can't begin to describe how heartbreaking it was to see my son's little body, lying motionless in a hospital bed, being hooked up to all kinds of tubes and not being able to do anything for him. My only recourse was to pray for him, and let me assure you, I did this constantly.

Then, one night my prayers were answered, literally. While I was beside my son's bed, asking God for help, I heard a voice that was as clear and real as any voice ever could be. It was as though someone was right beside me, telling me, "When you get meningitis, your brain swells and presses against the skull, and that's what causes brain damage. Your son will be okay, and he won't get brain damage."

This answer was an enormous comfort to me and gave me hope that my son would indeed by okay.

Over the next week, my son's condition improved. The doctor treating him sat me down and explained what happens when you have the meningitis bug. It was exactly the words I heard in my mind just nights before. He told me about how the brain swells and how it can cause damage, but the swelling my son experienced didn't seem to cause any damage. Personally, I feel like God made my son with a large head in order to protect him during this critical time.

Although my son was in the hospital for nearly six months and his full recovery took almost two years, as he eventually improved, he was just as bright and intelligent as before this terrible virus attacked his little body. Thankfully, he is fine today. In fact, he is the author of this book.

Carole B. - Australia

With God's Help, You Can Do Anything

Whether your heart's desire is emotional, physical, financial, spiritual, or anything else, I assure you that, with God's help, you can achieve greatness. If you want a better job, God can help you find one. If you need more money, God can help you get it. If you want more peace and happiness in your home, God can give it to you. No matter what you're looking to accomplish, with God on your side, you can achieve greatness. You can reach a level that is above and beyond anything you could ever do on your own.

2. *You Need to Ask For What You Want*

Hockey legend, Wayne Gretzky said, "You miss 100 percent of the shots you don't take"? Well, this is certainly applicable when it comes to unleashing more of God's blessings. You simply have to take a shot, or, in other words, you have to ask. Now, as obvious as this may sound, it's truly surprising just how many people fail to do this. They simply don't ask God to come into their lives and bless them. As a result, they miss out on receiving the things that God would have otherwise given. Allow me to further explain by sharing a personal story.

About ten years ago, I had the misfortune of having to attend traffic school. While there, the instructor told us about a conversation he recently had with a traffic officer. He asked the officer if he ever let people off with a warning instead of giving them a ticket.

The officer said, "If they ask, I almost always give people a warning instead of a ticket. But most people don't ask for a warning, so I mostly write tickets."

After sharing this story, many of the traffic school participants, including myself, expressed remorse at not having asked for a warning. But none of us knew we could have potentially avoided getting a ticket by simply asking. If we did, we certainly would have asked.

In a similar manner, many of us fail to receive blessings from God because we simply don't ask for them. For whatever reason, we just don't take the time to kneel down in prayer and ask God to bless us with the things we most want. Unfortunately though, it's unlikely that God will bless you with the abundance that we've been discussing until you do so. It's as simple as that. Receiving blessings from God requires that you ask, and prayer is the perfect place to do this.

THIS IS MY CHILD, TOO!

My wife and I had tried for such a long time to get pregnant. So now that she was a few hours from delivering our first child, we were absolutely thrilled. We were having a little boy, and things were going great. Or at least we thought they were. Our little boy's heart rate had suddenly fallen below a safe level. Although the nurses had turned my wife from side to side, nothing they seemed to do helped. Eventually, the doctor ordered that my wife be taken to surgery for an emergency C-section.

I was instructed to put on some scrubs and a mask, and I was led into an operating room where I saw nurses rigorously applying some kind of antiseptic to my wife's stomach. Everyone in the room seemed to know their jobs. They all looked calm, but this wasn't any comfort.

All at once, several thoughts entered my mind. I thought about how much I loved my wife. I thought about how much I loved my unborn son. Most of all, I thought about how it was my job to protect them and in this situation, there was absolutely nothing I could do.

I quickly said a silent prayer and asked God to make everything okay. Almost immediately, I felt an assurance that everything was going to be all right and the situation would resolve itself. However, more than that, I felt like God Himself whispered to my soul and said something that I'll never forget. He said, "Don't forget. This is my child, too. I'll be watching over him."

I can't tell you how strange I felt. On one hand, my wife was about to be cut open. On the other hand, I was feeling overjoyed that God was aware of my situation and He had assured me that everything was going to be fine.

Then, with the scalpel in hand and within moments of cutting into my wife, the doctor paused and said, "Let's give it ten more seconds, if your baby's heart rate doesn't go up, we'll go in." My son's heart rate did go up, and a C-section wasn't necessary after all. The situation did indeed resolve itself and a few hours later, my son was born.

That night, I thanked God for helping my family and giving us a child. Most of all, I thanked Him for reminding me that He is my Father, and the Father of us all. Because of this, He has just as much an interest in my life and the life of my children, as I do.

Jason T. - Georgia

You may be wondering why God doesn't just give people what they need or want without them having to ask. He clearly already knows what these things are, so why can't He just snap His fingers and make them happen? Although we will discuss this question more thoroughly later, for now, please know that God is your loving and completely wise Father. As such, He knows everything about you and wants the very best for you. He understands that, in order for you to reach your full potential, you need to work for the things you get.

Although you may have never thought about it this way, but prayer is actually a form of work. When you put in the time and effort to pray, it demonstrates to God that you are willing to work for the things you want. Then, when you have done your part, God will do His, and this collective effort allows for miracles to occur and truly magnificent things to happen. So go ahead, take your shot, and ask God to bless you.

> *If you really want God to bless you in abundance... you need to know what He looks for when answering your prayers.*

3. *There Are Rules to Prayer*

Have you ever wondered how an airplane flies, or perhaps how a television works? What about your computer or your digital camera? How do they work? I ask because I want to point out that, for the most part, we take for granted the wonders of technology and just use whatever we have at our disposal. And that's okay. After all, you don't need to know how electricity works in order to benefit from turning on a light. Likewise, you don't need to know how God answers prayers in order to have your prayers answered. Right? Well, yes and no.

Sure, having faith in the process of prayer without understanding everything about prayer is perfectly fine. However, if you really want God to help you achieve greatness, then it's important to know more than just how to flip a switch. You need to know what God looks for when answering your prayers. You need to know the rules of prayer.

The rules of prayer are more than just suggestions as to how you might approach God. They are the actual guidelines and principles that, if followed, will help you create a life where God will more readily pour out more of his magnificent blessings. If you want better relationships, a better job, better communication skills, financial security, a nicer house, or anything else, following the rules of prayer will enable God to bless you with everything that you both want and need.

So what exactly are the rules of prayer?

Well, I assure you they are not complicated, but I want to give them their proper examination. Therefore, I will postpone giving the specifics of these rules until later. Until then, just know that, when I refer to the rules of prayer, I am referring to the rules that govern your ability to have your prayers answered and for God to bless you with greatness.

4. *God Wants You to Be Happy*

When you think about all the things with which God can bless you, it can be rather exhilarating. After all, God can grant any of your heart's desires. He can give you riches, fame, power, wisdom, or any other thing. But, even though the extent of what He can give you is unlimited, have you ever stopped and considered what He wants to give you? Instead of telling Him what you want, have you ever considered what God wants you to have?

Does He want you to have a new car or a new job? Does He want you to be incredibly rich or powerful? Maybe. In fact, He may even help you get these things. But I'm not convinced that getting a new car or being rich is what God put you on earth to exclusively do. Rather, more than any other thing, God wants you to be happy.

Let me say that again. God wants you to be happy!

He wants you to experience all of the joy that life can offer. The magnificent relationships, the opportunities to grow and learn, the joy of serving others, the peace that comes from living His commandments, the exhilaration of reaching your full potential. These are the things that bring true happiness and like any loving father, God wants you to experience them. He wants you to be happy.

THE DAY I BECAME A FATHER... AGAIN

I was probably in my mid-thirties at the time. I had three young children, and I worked very hard. Every day, I would leave my home at five o'clock in the morning, and I wouldn't get home until around eight o'clock that night. I never really saw my home in the daytime, and I was completely caught up in the acquisition of things.

One day, as I was getting ready to leave for work, the earth began to shake in a way that I'll never forget. It was the morning of January 17, 1994, and we were living in Northridge, California. I felt like the world was going to cave in and collapse on us. We lived in this ranch-style home with wooden floors, and all you could hear was the sound of glass crashing and things falling off the walls. There was so much noise.

I quickly ran to get my three-year-old son and tucked him under my arm. My wife ran through the house, across the floor that was full of glass and debris, and got our other two children. Then, as the earth shook, I gathered my family together hoping to find safety.

As the world was crashing down upon us, the thing I thought to do was to pray. I put my arms around my family and asked God to protect us. As I offered this prayer, a peace came to my mind and I knew everything would be all right.

Afterward, the thought occurred to me that it took a 6.7 earthquake to get me where I really needed to be, on my knees, praying with my arms around my family. Yes, many of our possessions were gone. So much of what had seemed so important was smashed. However, that day, I came to know in a very real way that nothing was more important than my family, and kneeling with them in prayer is perhaps the best thing I could ever do.

The earthquake that day destroyed so very much, but I don't remember it for that. I remember it as the day that I became a father again.

Mark A. - California

As you embark upon your journey to learning the secrets of prayer, please know that all of your petitions and desires will be subject to God's ultimate purpose for you, which is for you to be happy. The great part about this is that true happiness is typically accomplished when you work hard and achieve your goals, when you serve others, when you spend time with your family, and when you do what is right. And these things are what Jesus referred to in Matthew as "being good" and are therefore eligible for God's divine assistance.

So when you think about all the things that God can give you, think about what He wants to give you. Chances are that you and He probably want the same things. For you to be happy.

Prayer is one of the most incredible tools that God has given us. Although often misunderstood and certainly under-utilized, prayer can allow God to bless your life in a way like nothing else can. Best of all, God has promised that, as you come to Him in prayer, your requests will be heard and answered. Just remember the words that Jesus said in Matthew that we quoted earlier.

> *And whatever you ask in prayer, you will receive, if you have faith.*
>
> (Matt 21:22)

God wants to bless you with greatness. He wants you to tap into His awesome power for the things that you both need and want. While it's true that God helps those who help themselves, helping yourself means learning about and immersing yourself in the powerful, magnificent, and awesome process of prayer.

I promise that, as you do this and follow the steps outlined in the chapters to come, you will learn the secrets of prayer and know exactly what it will take for God to bless your life with all of the abundance, prosperity, and happiness that you could ever hope for.

Your life can be extraordinary. You can achieve greatness and it begins with developing a better relationship with your God through prayer.

Key Principles to Remember

- Because God loves you, He wants to bless you. He will go to great lengths to help you achieve all of your goals, regardless of how lofty or extravagant they might seem.
- Many of us fail to receive blessings from God because we simply don't take the time to pray and ask God for the exact things we want. However, having God bless you more abundantly requires that you ask, and prayer is a place where you can do this.
- If you really want to call upon the powers of Heaven and achieve greatness, then it's important to know what God looks for when answering your prayers. You need to know the rules of prayer.
- More than any other thing, as I have been stressing, God wants you to be happy. He wants you to experience all of the joy that life can offer— the magnificent relationships, the opportunities to grow and learn, and the peace that comes from living in a manner that is pleasing to Him.

CHAPTER TWO

THE NATURE OF GOD

God loves each of us as if there were only one of us.

St. Augustine

What God Is Really Like

To understand why God wants to help you achieve greatness, it's important to first know more about who He is and what He is like. For some, God represents something abstract, distant, and out-of-touch. For others, God represents a beautiful and loving Father who is all-powerful and completely aware of everything we do and everything we think. But which view is right? What is God really like?

In answering this question, the first thing you must realize is that God loves you very much, and this loves serves as the foundation for everything He does. Every decision He makes, every action He takes, and every blessing He bestows is based upon His incredible, unconditional, and overwhelming love. Because of this love, He will go to great lengths to ensure you are getting all you need in order to reach your full potential, grow and learn, and be happy. Indeed, God loves you and all of His children, and this infinite capacity to love defines what God is really like.

The Call No Parent Wants

Every night, I pray for the safety of each of my children, and I have faith that God will protect them. After finishing my prayers one night, I went to bed and fell asleep. A few hours later, the phone woke me up, and I immediately knew that something was wrong. It was the hospital, informing me that my daughter had been involved in a head-on collision with a drunk driver. My heart stopped! Instinctively, I feared the worst.

Fortunately, these fears weren't realized. The person on the other end of the phone informed me that my daughter was alive and she was going to be okay. However, my daughter's car had rolled over several times, during which her hand had been forced out of her window and completely crushed.

My husband and I made our way to the emergency room to see our daughter. Thankfully, she was alive and expected to make a full recovery. But that's just the first part of the story.

Following my daughter that night was a couple who, upon seeing the accident, stopped to help. They immediately noticed that my daughter's hand had been crushed. As luck would have it, the driver of this car was a hand surgeon. He quickly administered to my daughter, and the very things he did, in all likelihood, helped save her hand.

Then the next car that stopped was on off-duty police officer who was able to coordinate getting the highway patrol and paramedics to the scene in record time. This also helped in the aid of our daughter, as well as the other driver. But it didn't stop there. Upon arriving at the hospital, a world-renowned surgeon greeted my daughter. He just happened to be on call that night. In operating, he used unprecedented surgical techniques that will help my daughter regain full use of her hand.

In looking back, I don't think the couple following my daughter, the off-duty police officer, or the emergency room surgeon helped my daughter by coincidence. Instead, I'm convinced that God guided them to assist her as an answer to my prayers.

My husband and I had prayed that our children would be safe. Although my daughter was a little banged up, she was safe. My loving Heavenly Father put people in her life at the exact moment she needed, and I am so grateful for that.

Judy K. - California

Understanding God's Love

If you're anything like me, appreciating the extent and depth of God's loves is a lot easier said than done. Let me explain.

Even though my parents taught me about my Heavenly Father from an early age and their teachings seemed to only reinforce what I innately knew to be true (that God is real), I must admit there have been times when I have questioned how God can love each and every person in the world, particularly me. With so many billions of other children to worry about, what makes me special enough to garner God's individual attention and be a recipient of His personal love? At least that's how I've sometimes felt. Let me tell about such a time.

During my freshman year of college, I began to question if God understood my personal struggles and challenges, and whether He really loved me. Now don't get me wrong. I didn't question if God was aware of my situation or even if He loved His children, at least collectively. Rather, I wondered if He cared about my situation and loved me individually. I was studying thousands of miles away from home, and was at a point in my life where I desperately needed to feel God's love, and know that

He cared. Above all, I wanted the reassurance that I wasn't alone, and that I could face my challenges with my Father by my side. However, pray as I might, I couldn't seem to silence my doubts. In fact, the more I prayed, the more I struggled with the idea that God really cared about me as an individual.

Fortunately, even though I wasn't feeling like I was making any progress, God was preparing a way for me to receive the answers and comfort I was looking for. And you know what? That's often how God works when you pray. You may not feel as though He is listening or helping when in reality He is. In fact, the very moment you ask for something, God starts the process of answering your prayers by orchestrating a way for you to receive the exact thing you're looking for. Just because you can't see what God is doing directly, that doesn't mean He isn't putting things together in a behind-the-scenes sort of way. That's certainly what He did for me.

It was Christmas Eve and I had been invited to a family dinner with my college roommate, Joe. I knew Joe's family very well and I was really excited to be with them for this special occasion.

After feasting upon a wonderful dinner, Joe's grandmother, invited me to sit next to her on the sofa and look through a large photo album. I gladly accepted this invitation, not knowing that doing so, would give me the answers that I was so desperately seeking.

As this lovely woman turned the pages of the album, she would sigh and say something so wonderful and so unique about each person in each photo. There must have been at least twenty grandchildren and just as many great-grandchildren. I was impressed by how this remarkable woman knew all of her family members intimately and how proud she was of them.

Then, completely unexpectedly, she said something that totally changed my outlook on my relationship with God and answered the very question with which I had been struggling. She said, "Even though I am a mother, grandmother, and great-grandmother to so many, I know all of my children, and I love them." She then went on to say something that hit me with such force and power that it felt like God Himself had told her what to say.

She said, "Having this love for my family lets me know that God loves me and that He loves all of us."

There it was, the answer I had been looking for. I finally knew how it was possible for God to love me as an individual.

One by one, God personally created us and we are, literally, His sons and daughters. That's how He can love us both collectively and, most important, individually. He knows us. He knows you!

God is able to love you and me for the same reason that Joe's grandmother was able to love each and every person in her family. Not only had she personally raised many of them, but she was also completely interwoven into their lives as well as the lives of her grandchildren and great-grandchildren. She had spent her life helping them, caring for them, and loving them. She had attended countless baseball games, soccer games, piano recitals, school plays, birthday parties, baptisms, family dinners, and so on. She had laughed with them, cried with them, and watched them learn and grow. She could unequivocally declare her love for her entire family, regardless of how many there were, because she knew them. All of them!

It's the same with God. One by one, He personally created us and we are, literally, His sons and daughters. That's how He can love us both collectively and, most important, individually. He knows us! All of us! Just consider what God said to the prophet Jeremiah.

> *Before I formed you in the womb I knew you, and before you were born I consecrated you; I appointed you a prophet to the nations.*
>
> (Jeremiah 1:5)

This Scripture suggests that, before being born physically, God knew about us and what our personalities would be like. What our individual talents would be, what challenges we would have, and everything else about our life. That's how He can love us individually. He really does know us.

Much like Joe's grandmother, who loved all of her family because she knew them, God loves you for the same reason. He knows you!

I Truly Am God's Daughter

Like many parents, I often check on my kids while they're sleeping, to make sure they're okay. After doing this one night, I was preparing for bed myself and like I normally do, I got down on my knees and started to pray. Now sometimes when I pray, I'm really good about focusing and saying exactly the right things. However on this particular night, my thoughts were all over the place, and thank goodness they were.

During this prayer, when I was supposed to be talking with my Heavenly Father, I was thinking about my kids and how much I loved them. I was replaying events in my mind about things they had done and said. Overall, I was just having a good time thinking about how lucky I was to have such beautiful children.

I tried a few times to get back on track with my prayer, but I soon figured that this prayer just wasn't going to happen and I needed to go to bed. That's when I had a truly wonderful experience. One I will never forget.

Just as I was about to finish my prayer, a thought came into my mind that literally changed the way I look at things.

The way in which I check on my children at night was similar to the way in which God checks in on me. Without my knowing it, He is constantly watching over me and making sure I'm okay.

At that moment, my understanding of my real relationship to God became very clear. I was truly His daughter, and just like I love my children, God loves me. He is concerned about my life, is aware of who I am, and what I am doing.

Now when I check on my kids at night, I think about how God loves me and constantly checks on me, too. I am so grateful that I understand who God really is. He is my loving Father, and I am His daughter.

Michelle H. - Idaho

God Made You in His Image

Have you ever wondered what God looks like? What about His personality, what's it like? Well, the Scriptures tell us that God created man in His own image.

> *Then God said, "Let us make man in our image, after our likeness."*
>
> (Genesis 1:26)

But why is this so important, and what does it mean? Simply

put, it means that God looks like us, or, more accurately, we look like God. But more than just being physically similar to God, we are also emotionally similar, and this is critical to understand. You see, if God were just some kind of mystical being, or energy force, (like many believe,) there's no way that He could relate to you or understand the range of human emotions that you experience.

He wouldn't know what grief, joy, or love was like. He wouldn't know about happiness, sadness, excitement, or anticipation. But, fortunately, that's not the case. God does understand what you're going through because He is similar to us. Or, as stated, we are similar to Him.

Think about it like this. We know that when Jesus was on earth, He experienced every possible human emotion. He suffered, cried, anguished. He was tempted, betrayed and persecuted. He also experienced joy and happiness. Surely, no one is more qualified on the human condition than Jesus. And doesn't Jesus declare that He and the Father are one?

Therefore, when you pray, you should picture God like you picture Jesus. As a real person, with real thoughts and real feelings. God can relate to everything you do and say, everything you have experienced, and everything you will experience.

God Knows Everything About Everything

Whether you've realized it or not, God is with you and watching over your every step. He is aware of all that you do, and He will go to great lengths to ensure your happiness and well-being. He is indeed your Father, and you are indeed His child. However, more than just being any kind of Father, God is a perfect Father who is always looking out for your best interests. He can always be counted on to do everything right. He is perfectly honest, fair, and just. And to top it off, He is all-knowing.

Just think about what Matthew 10:29–31 says:

Are not two sparrows sold for a penny? And not on[e] them will fall to the ground apart from your Father.

But even the hairs of your head are all numbered.

Fear not, therefore; you are of more value than many sparrows.

God does indeed know everything about everything. If you have a broken heart or a peaceful mind, God is aware of it. If your life is a stormy sea or blissful meadow, He knows about it. He rejoices in all of your victories and anguishes in all of your defeats. He can see things and understand things that you can't, and He uses this foresight to bless your life in ways that you simply can't comprehend. He is there to help, guide, and comfort you.

Best of all, God is the Father who is always available, forever dependable. He has never been, nor will He ever be, an absentee Father. When you call out to Him or need His help, He literally drops everything to respond to your every concern, thought, or request. Never mind that it is nearly impossible to understand how He does this. Just know that He does.

The next time you pray, imagine you're literally walking and talking with God. He is eager to listen to you, help you, comfort you, and guide you.

What's Important to You Is Important to God

Because God loves you, whatever is important to you is important to Him. It simply doesn't matter what else is occurring- wars, floods, or famine, your personal world is just as much a concern to God as it is to you.

For example, think about the wedding in the village of Cana. The wine supply ran out during the festivities and Jesus' mother came to Him with the problem. Although Jesus said it wasn't yet time for miracles, He turned the water into wine because He knew it was important to His mother. Likewise, if something is important to you, much like Jesus responded to Mary's request, God will respond to you.

I Felt Like God Had Abandoned Us

My husband and I really wanted a baby. However, after five years of trying, we couldn't seem to get pregnant. We considered options like IVF, but, after thinking and praying about everything, we felt as though the best thing for us was to adopt.

I had prayed extensively that I would be able to get pregnant. And, interestingly, almost every time I did pray, I felt like it was going to happen. I just needed to be patient and have faith. However, after not getting pregnant for so many years, I started to lose hope. I have to admit that my prayers confused me. Was I misinterpreting my feelings? Was God really saying that, instead of giving birth to my own child, I would be a mother to an adopted child? I didn't know anymore. I just wanted a child and I didn't care if he were naturally mine or not.

To our surprise, the adoption process was very quick. After only a few months of being on the list, a young girl had seen our profile and decided she wanted us to be the parents of her child. Finally, we were going to be parents! I can't even describe how excited we were, but unfortunately, our excitement was short-lived.

When the time of delivery was only a few weeks away, to our absolute shock and total heartbreak, the mother of this little baby decided against the adoption. She wanted to raise the child herself. Although we were happy for her, we were both completely devastated. I felt like God had totally abandoned us.

However, just when you think all hope is lost and no one is there for you, God has a way of letting you know that He really is there, and He really does care. In this time of total turmoil, something remarkable happened. After trying for so many years to have a baby and then being so disappointed about the adoption not working out, I got pregnant. My husband and I were going to have a child of our own. Once the disbelief had worn off, we were ecstatic!

Looking back, God didn't abandon me. He was always there with His arms wrapped tightly around me. The feelings of peace and assurance I had felt so many times when I had prayed and asked God to help us get pregnant weren't wrong. I didn't misinterpret them. My timing was just off.

I now have four children, the youngest of whom was adopted. My life is so full and I have so many blessings, all thanks to my loving Father in Heaven.

Jennifer K. - Virginia

Walking With God

Because God is your Father and you are His child, when you pray, you can talk to Him like you would a beloved and trusted parent, grandparent, friend, or mentor. Be personal and intimate with Him. Share the details of your life with Him, the highs and lows, the victories and the failures. Allow yourself to develop a deep and everlasting bond with Him. It's not that God doesn't know all these things about you already, it's that He wants and expects to hear from you. He wants you to take the time to get to know Him, like He knows you.

When you pray, it's important to keep in mind how much God loves you and this love should set the tone for your prayer. Personally, to help me do this, sometimes before I pray, I picture myself walking side by side with God. Sometimes, we're walking along a beach. Sometimes, we're on a mountain trail or some other type of natural setting. As we walk, I envision what a conversation with God might be like under these circumstances and try to keep in mind that I'm in the presence of someone who loves me more than I can comprehend.

Doing this, or "walking with God" so to speak, is an extremely effective way for me to prepare for prayer. It not only reminds me that I am talking with my actual Father who loves me very much, but it also allows me to treat my prayers more like real conversations. I'm not the only one talking. I'm listening, too.

So, perhaps the next time you kneel down to pray, as you close your eyes, imagine you're literally walking and talking with God. If you do this, remember that He is eager to listen to you, help you, comfort you, and guide you. That's because He loves you. That's the nature of God.

As you take the time to get to know God and begin to reveal yourself to Him through prayer, something very interesting happens. God, in turn, reveals Himself to you.

Developing a Relationship With God Takes Work

As you've probably figured out by now, prayer isn't so much for God, as it is for you. It can make your life better than it otherwise would be, but it involves your making an effort to get to know God. You are required to do your part!

Think about it like this. Have you ever had a wonderful relationship with a person who you don't visit, call, or pay any attention to? I sincerely doubt it. That's because relationships take nurturing. You can't expect to be someone's friend or even their acquaintance if you never do anything to actually nurture that friendship. It's the same with you and your Heavenly Father. Unless you put in the effort to know God, you're simply not going to have a personal relationship with Him, and not having a personal relationship with God is far more detrimental for you than it is for Him.

Keep in mind though, even when you fail to call out to God and even if you're doing things that are wrong, He is still there for you. He still loves you, and He will still bless you. However, the full extent of His blessings are reserved for those who do call out to Him, listen to what He says, and follow His commandments.

The Awesome Side Benefit of Prayer

As you take the time to get to know God and begin to reveal yourself to Him through prayer, something very interesting happens. God, in turn, reveals Himself to you. Without any extra effort on your part, God brings you closer and closer into compliance with His will, and this is one of the most remarkable by-products of prayer. Little by little, you progress and improve. Your nature evolves, and you become more like the person God wants you to be. This in turn allows God to more fully bless your life.

We Both Got What We Wanted

It was the second time I was going to take the exam for medical school. The first time I took the exam, my results weren't good enough to be considered for the schools I wanted to attend. This time, however, I was determined to do better. Not only was my preparation going to be better, but also my prayers were going to be better. I figured I had tried to do it on my own, and that hadn't worked out. So now, I was going to ask God to help me.

Before every study session, I prayed and asked God to bless me. That my mind might be open to learning new things and that I would remember what I had studied. When I said my prayers at night, I asked for the motivation and dedication to work and study as hard as I could. Mostly, I asked God to help me in the actual test, remember what I had studied, and be able to work quickly and efficiently.

The night before the test, although I felt like my preparation was sufficient, I was still nervous. I offered a prayer and asked God to bless me and help me in my exam. As I was praying, I started to feel very relaxed and at complete peace. It was a very comforting feeling. As I continued to pray, I got the sense that God was aware of my efforts and He would help me in the exam.

The next day, I took the exam. Although I didn't breeze through it, I truly felt like God was watching over me and helping me remember things. As I was taking the test, I felt calm, relaxed, and at peace. I knew God was watching over me and my efforts were better because of it.

When my test results came back, I had received high enough scores to warrant interviews from the schools I wanted. I was overcome with joy, and I thanked God for helping me. This was an amazing experience for me, and it helped me know just how much God loves me and is willing to help so long as I ask Him to. It also allowed me to come closer to God than I had ever been. I think that's a real win-win.

James S. - New York

Now, even though God is perfect and we are imperfect, God accepts our humanness and loves us for who we are. He knows we're going to mess up and make mistakes, and He provided a way whereby we can overcome these mistakes. Because of His everlasting love for us, He sent us His Son to pay for our sins. By believing in Jesus we can become perfect.

> *For God so loved the world, that he gave his only Son, that whoever believes in him should not perish but have eternal life.*
>
> (John 3:16)

Missing the Mark

Think about it like this. The Greek definition of the word "sin" can be translated to "missing the mark." When we do what is wrong, God completely understands that we're human. Best of all, He is always there to help us get back on track. Repeatedly, He reaches down and lifts us up. God never, not for one second, turns His back on us or stops loving us.

What an awesome thing to know! Regardless of how much you display your humanness or how much you "miss the mark," God always love you. He always has, and He always will. His love for you is unconditional and absolute. In knowing this, you should never feel awkward or ashamed to approach God in prayer. He will always listen, be there, and help. His arms are forever extended, inviting you to come to Him.

If you're not seeing the results of God's blessings in every area of your life, then your relationship with God might need tweaking.

More than likely, you just need to put a little more time into developing this relationship.

As you do, you will get to know God better. In turn, you will automatically start doing more of what God wants you to, and this will make you more eligible for God's blessings.

If you are at a crossroads right now, wanting God to take over the welfare of your life, I invite you to approach Him in humble prayer. Experience the awesome nature of His love! Wrap your mind around the fact that God is literally your Father and you are literally His child. He knows you individually because you are His creation! And best of all, He loves you, and He does so (and I repeat) unconditionally.

Key Principles to Remember

- God loves you very much, and this loves serves as the foundation for everything He does.
- When you pray, you should picture God for what He is: your very real, very tangible, perfect Father. He can relate to everything you do and say, everything you have experienced and everything you will experience.
- One by one, God personally created us. We are, literally, His sons and daughters. That's how He can love us both collectively and, most important, individually.
- God is with you and watching over your every step. He is aware of all that you do, and He will go to great lengths to ensure your happiness and well-being
- Unless you put in the effort it takes to truly know God, you're not going to have a personal relationship with Him. It's that simple. And not having that intimate relationship is far more detrimental for you than it is for Him.
- Above all, remember this: God's love is unconditional. You should never feel awkward or ashamed to approach Him in prayer. He will always listen and be there to help.

Chapter Three

What Do Most People Want from God?

Call to me and I will answer you.

Jeremiah 33:3

Dad, Can I Get Whatever I Want?

A few years ago, a friend invited my then nine-year-old son and me to a Major League baseball game. Although I had taken my son to many games in the past, this game was going to be different. Instead of sitting in one of the many thousands of general seats throughout the stadium, like we usually did, my friend had invited us to join him in his luxury suite.

After arriving at the game, my friend gave us a rundown of his suite. He showed us where to get food and drinks (of which there seem to be an unlimited supply). He showed us where we could sit and made us feel very welcome.

After being at the game for a little while, my son leaned to me and asked, "Can I get some nachos?" I said, "Sure." After eating those, he asked, "Can I get a hot dog?" I said, "Go for it." Next, he somewhat hesitantly asked, "Can I have a hamburger?"

When I quickly said yes, he looked puzzled and asked, "Dad, can I get whatever I want?"

I told him, "Yes. You can."

With a big smile, he then proceeded to take full advantage of my friend's generosity. In fact, I don't think I've ever seen him eat so much food or have such a good time at a ball game. The only disappointing part of the evening was that our team, the Angels, lost to the Rangers.

Driving home that night, I found myself reflecting on the game and the overall experience of being there with my son. I smiled to myself when I pictured the look of excitement on his face when he realized he could get "whatever he wanted."

In a similar way, the question my son asked at that game that night is one that many of us often ask God. "Dad, can I get whatever I want?" However, instead of asking for food, like my son had, we ask God about a whole host of other things that affect our lives, like our finances, jobs, families, health, and so on. We want to know if God can help us with whatever we want.

Just because something seems impossible to you, that doesn't mean it's impossible for God. He can intervene in your life at any time, at any place, and for any reason.

God Cares About What You Want

Much like any loving parent would go to extraordinary lengths to help their children achieve their goals and be happy, your loving Heavenly Father will do the same for you. Whether you're looking for help to start a business, pay the bills, get along with your kids, feel more of God's love, get in better physical shape, or anything else, you can be assured that, not only does God know about what you want, but He also cares about it too.

Therefore, when you approach God with your wants and needs, keep in mind that, like any loving parent, as your Heavenly Parent, He wants to help you. Best of all, because He is all-powerful, anything is possible. If getting something requires some tinkering on His behalf, He can do it. Any help you want or need, no matter what it is or how impossible it might seem, God can provide.

Just think about with His infinite power, He can make anything happen. Just think about what He did for the prophet Gideon in the Old Testament.

Gideon was called to deliver the Israelites from bondage. To do this, he was given the daunting task of going against 135,000 Midianite soldiers with only 300 of his own men. Sure, the odds weren't in his favor, but God wanted it that way. That's because God wanted to make sure that the Israelites (and everyone else for that matter) knew He delivered Gideon's people out of bondage and He (God) could do anything.

As the story goes, Gideon marched his three hundred men to the Midianite camp and defeated them with nothing more than torches and trumpets. Gideon and his men were triumphant because God used His infinite power to intervene in the situation. There is absolutely no doubt that without God's help, Gideon's men would not have seized this miraculous victory.

In a like manner, God can intervene in your life in any way, at any time, and for any reason. He will be there for you, ready to help whenever you call upon Him. Furthermore, as the Gideon story highlights, when God does something, He can do it in a truly spectacular manner and can make things happen that just otherwise wouldn't. Just because something seems impossible to you, that doesn't mean it's impossible for God. In fact, no matter what you're looking to accomplish, God can help you do it.

Plus, keep in mind that, when God does intervene in your life to make something happen, it's really easy for Him to do so. It's important to start thinking about garnering God's help from this perspective.

The Kid Scissors

Recently, my six-year-old daughter asked me to get the kid scissors down from the top of the fridge so she could cut some paper. Because she wasn't tall enough to reach them on her own, she simply asked for my help. Being her loving mom, I was obviously more than happy to get them.

As I was praying that night, I thought about the situation earlier that day with my daughter. Even though it wasn't difficult for me to help her, I was impressed at how grateful she was that I did. Her thanks seemed to be almost too much. All I did was reach up on the fridge and get her the scissors. Then I thought about it from my daughter's perspective. Without me, she couldn't have completed her paper-cutting task, and that would have been very frustrating for her. I then thought about my relationship with God and about all the things I needed Him to do that I couldn't do on my own.

After all, for God, my requests are probably a lot like getting kid scissors down from the top of the fridge. It's no big deal to Him, but everything to me.

Kerry A. - Nevada

What Do Most People Want From God?

For the most part, we tend to face similar trials. While the specific circumstances of these trials vary from person to person, the general nature of the difficulties we face, and things we want, are common to most people. That is why I have found that, although God can help us accomplish anything, most people ask God to help them in one (or all) of four situations. These are:

1. *Financial Security*
2. *Relationships*
3. *Health*
4. *Happiness*

Wealth can oftentimes be a by-product of God helping you achieve your goals and reach your full potential.

1. Having God Bless You Financially

Many years ago, I invested in a start-up company that I thought was going to be the next big thing. However, like many start-ups, the reality didn't live up to the hype, and I lost hundreds of thousands of dollars. As I tried to make sense of what had happened, I must admit that I considered the idea that God may not want me to be overly wealthy; that no matter what I did, my life was destined to be comfortable but not extravagant. Perhaps you have felt this way, too. And, like me, you may have even justified your thinking by suggesting that God is somehow protecting you from the money-related sins like pride, greed, and selfishness. After all, the Scriptures warn us of the dangers of being rich.

> *It is easier for a camel to go through the eye of a needle than for a rich person to enter the kingdom of God.*
>
> (Mark 10:25)

Considering this passage, it's easy to assume that God isn't going to help someone become rich and therefore purposefully decrease his chances of getting into heaven. Or, if God does decide to bless someone financially, then certainly there has to be a limit as to how much. Right? Well, not exactly.

While it's true that God has warned us in the book of Timothy about "the love of money being the root of all evil," that doesn't mean God won't bless you financially and do so in abundance. In fact, provided you follow the rules of prayer, God can bless you with almost anything you want, including wealth. And rest assured, if He does bless you with wealth, even vast wealth, you can still be eligible to enter His kingdom.

But how and when will God bless you financially? Before I reveal the answers to these very important questions, please keep two things in mind.

First, as you probably know, being rich (or being truly rich) is more about the quality of your life than the amount of money you have. For now though, as we discuss being rich, let's do so from a purely financial perspective.

Second, one person's definition of being rich can be very different from another person's. We all have different ways of looking at the world and different experiences that have shaped our opinions. For example, some people might consider being rich as having a certain amount of money and living a luxurious lifestyle. For others, being rich may simply be having money left over at the end of the month after all the bills are paid. Whatever your definition, I think you should consider some particulars.

Typically, we need a certain amount of money every month to survive. We need to buy food and clothes and make rent or mortgage payments. We need to pay utility bills, car payments, insurance premiums, credit cards bills, and a variety of other expenses. For many people, it can be extremely hard to make ends meet. For those of us who have struggled to pay the bills at some point in our lives, or who are struggling right now, the question isn't, "Can God help me be rich?" It's, "Can God help me pay the bills this month?"

There should be absolutely no doubt as to whether or not God wants to help you when it comes to your everyday financial needs. He is intimately aware of all your personal monetary obligations, and He will give to you liberally when you ask. In fact, God is so concerned about your everyday financial needs that He'll even help you overcome situations that are completely your own fault. If you've overextended yourself or put yourself in too much debt, God can help you find a way out. That doesn't mean you'll avoid the consequences of your actions, but it does mean that God will help you find a way to dig yourself out of whatever mess you are in, no matter how dire.

I Couldn't Do It without God

A few years ago, I refinanced my house into one of those new loan programs that featured a very small, up-front interest rate. I figured the savings I would enjoy during the introductory low teaser rate would be more than enough to make up for any future interest rate hikes or decline in the housing market. I was certain that in just a few years, I would be ahead financially. Well, that was the plan, but, unfortunately, the plan didn't work out the way I wanted.

From the time I took out this loan to the time I needed to refinance it, the housing market crashed. When my teaser rate was up, the interest on my loan went up, too. To make matters worse, the value of my house was now less than what I owed, and my new payments were practically impossible for me to make. I decided to see if the bank would modify my loan, and I submitted a modification application. Unfortunately, the bank denied my request. Now I really didn't know what to do.

How could this have happened? I was normally so responsible with my finances, but now my greed had put me in a situation that seemed hopeless. I really needed help. My poor decisions had put my family at risk, and I was embarrassed and ashamed to approach God with this problem.

I eventually swallowed my pride and asked God to help me. I felt like I should resubmit my modification application, but, this time, I would combine my application with some very intense prayers. As I prayed, I pleaded with God to help soften the hearts of the people in charge of my modification. I also promised God that I would not be so foolish or greedy in the future with respect to my finances.

After many months, I got word that my bank had agreed to modify my loan. When I finished reading the e-mail that outlined the terms of my new loan, I felt an overwhelming sense of gratitude to God for helping me. I knew my prayers had made the difference. I immediately got on my knees and thanked God for His help. By myself, I couldn't accomplish what I wanted, but, with God, I did.

Joel G. - Oregon

Can God Help You Be Rich?

God is more than willing to help you with your everyday financial needs, but, more than just helping you get by, God can go beyond this. In fact, He can use His infinite and matchless power to help you achieve any level of financial security and prosperity that you desire. But under what circumstances will He help you do this?

Before I answer this, please let me point out something that's really important. While God certainly cares about everything in our lives, the extent to which He cares about your being rich is questionable. That's because God didn't put you here for the sole purpose of helping you become rich. Instead, His main priority is for you to be happy and reach your full potential, and He knows exactly what it takes for you to do this. It's when you do what is right, work hard, and achieve your goals.

If one of your goals happens to be financial in nature, like being a better businessperson, getting a promotion at work, or even having enough money to spend more time with your family, then getting rich can oftentimes be a by-product of God helping you achieve your goals and reach your full potential.

God can help you financially, all while avoiding the traps and pitfalls of letting money prevent you from entering His kingdom.

The bottom line is that God is okay with you being rich. In fact, He can even help you become so. Just think about the way in which He blessed King Solomon.

God appeared to Solomon one night in a dream and asked what he would most desire. Now although Solomon could have asked for anything, his only request was that he would be granted wisdom in order to better govern his people. Because of Solomon's unselfishness, God not only blessed him with wisdom, but also blessed him with even unfathomable riches, a long life, and victory over his enemies.

The point here is that God didn't hesitate for one second to bless Solomon with the riches of the world. His blessings suggest that God is totally okay with your being rich. Granted, Solomon didn't ask to be blessed with riches, but God gave them nonetheless. Likewise, provided you follow the rules of prayer, God won't hesitate to bless you with riches, either.

My Heavenly Business Partner

I remember the day I left the comfort of my high-paying corporate job to start my own business. I was so excited because, like many new business owners, I had high hopes of success. Also, like many new business owners, I hadn't given too much thought as to what running a business really meant.

It wasn't long until my savings account was empty; my retirement account was empty, and to get by, I was forced to tap into the equity in my home. Needless to say, things were very bleak.

During this time, however, I prayed fervently to God for help and included Him in all of my decisions. As I did this, my relationship with Him got very strong. Yes, I was broke, but my closeness to God made me feel like the richest person in the world.

Then, after going to the brink of financial disaster, things started to happen that defied explanation. I would literally pray for business one day and get it the next. Every time I really needed money, it somehow came. My prayers were allowing me to access God's power, and let me tell you, that's a pretty awesome thing to experience. Today, my business is flourishing and I am financially secure.

Looking back, my path to success was very bumpy, and at times unclear. However, I believe God wanted it that way so that I might involve Him more in my life. Because of my challenges, my relationship with God is better than ever, and I believe that is why He blesses me so much.

James A. - Kansas

In the chapters ahead, I will reveal the step-by-step process of asking for and receiving God's help to bless you with the desires of your heart. Therefore, if one of your goals is to prosper financially, I will show you the exact steps to having God help you do this, all while avoiding the traps and pitfalls of letting money prevent you from entering His kingdom.

2. *Having God Improve Your Relationships*

In thinking about how God can bless you with riches, I want you to decide if being rich is more important than deepening and perfecting the relationships with the people you love. Obviously it's not. Therefore you mustn't ever let your drive for money interfere with your need to develop better and more meaningful relationships. After all, there's no point in being rich if you're unhappy. On the other hand, there's nothing better than having God bless you financially and then being able to enjoy this prosperity with the people you love.

Fortunately, you don't have to choose between having riches and having incredible relationships. With God's help, you can have both. That's because God wants every area of your life to be extraordinary. Remember, He didn't put you here to be mediocre. Rather, He put you here to reach your full potential and experience the absolute most out of life. This includes your having wonderful relationships with all the people you love.

> *God can make bad relationships good and good relationships better. In fact, He can take any relationship, and make it fantastic.*

You may be in a relationship that's not going exactly the way you want. On the other hand, you may be in a relationship that's good, but you want to improve it. Either way, God can help! He can help make bad relationships good and good relationships better. In fact, He can take any relationship, even the most troubled one, and make it fantastic. He can help you improve any situation or circumstance. That's because, with God, nothing is impossible. Whatever your personal situation, if you invite God to help you, He will.

We Just Weren't in Love Anymore

My marriage was in trouble. No matter what I did, nothing seemed to make my husband happy. Truth be told, nothing he did seemed to make me happy either. We just weren't in love anymore.

I was convinced that our only option was to get a divorce. I figured I deserved to be happy and in a relationship that was full of romance and excitement. Or, at least, that's how I justified my thinking.

While this was going on, I was watching television one day and stopped on a channel where a woman was talking about her marriage. I don't know what church she belonged to, but I remember being impressed at how she spoke so lovingly about her husband and how much she admired and respected him. She concluded her remarks by encouraging couples to pray together and involve God in their lives. She was even bold enough to promise that, if couples would do this, they could overcome any trial and would develop a deep and abiding love for one another.

At first, I dismissed this woman's comments about praying together as a couple. I simply wasn't going to do that. However, one night, my husband and I got into a rather nasty fight, and we both said some pretty horrible things to each other. We were both angry, and neither one of us wanted to give in. After a long, awkward pause, my husband calmly said, "In the bottom of my heart, I want our marriage to work, but I don't think it can. I don't know if I can go on."

The finality of his tone, and what he said, shocked me. Sure, I had thought about a divorce, but now I knew he had too. At that moment, I was scared. I knew I didn't want a divorce. So with as much courage as I could muster, I said, "I think I know what can save our marriage." He skeptically looked at me and, without speaking, acknowledged that he wanted to hear what I had to say.

Not knowing how he would react, I quietly said, "I think that, if we pray together and ask God to help us, then we can save our marriage."

After what seemed like an eternity, he responded. Not with words, but with tears. We got down on our knees and said a prayer together. It was a simple but heartfelt plea to God to bless our marriage. That was over fifteen years ago. For the most part, we have prayed together every night since.

I know that prayer saved our marriage! It has given us the courage to humble ourselves, and the capacity to love each other in a way that we didn't think we could. Because of prayer, I see my husband the way God sees him. I love him unconditionally, support him, defend him, trust him, and long to be with him. I know my husband feels the same about me.

I wish I knew who the woman was on television that day. I would like to thank her and let her know that her words led us to prayer, and that has made all the difference.

Mindy B. - Virginia

Whether it's improving the relationship with your significant other, children, extended family, or any other person, most of us want our relationships to be the best they can be. God wants this, too. Any relationship you're looking to improve can be helped by asking God. He understands that some of the greatest happiness and joy that we can experience in this life can come through our relationships. He will provide you the inspiration, the humility, perhaps the healing, and, most important, the desire to make your relationships the best they can be.

3. *Asking God to Improve Your Health*

In Matthew 6:27, Jesus asks His disciples what I consider to be one of the most poignant questions in all of Scripture.

> *Which of you by being anxious can add a single hour to his span of life?*

As I have thought about this question, I am convinced that Jesus didn't ask it in a rhetorical manner. Instead, I believe He asked it to point out the fact that, with faith, our bodies have extraordinary capabilities. These capabilities include things like losing weight, overcoming depression, changing our dispositions, and even healing ourselves. But how do you go about accomplishing these miraculous things?

Ask and It Will Be Given to You

As mentioned previously, you need to ask God to bless you with whatever you're looking for. If you or a loved one is sick, if you need to change your attitude, overcome an addiction, heal your broken heart, or anything else that ails you, then simply ask God to help. Your prayers can literally summon the healing powers of heaven. Repeatedly, the Bible reveals how God will give us whatever we ask for. Probably the most famous of these passages is found in Matthew 7:7.

> *Ask, and it will be given to you; seek, and you will find; knock, and it will be opened to you.*

The point here is that, because God's power is unlimited, He can bless you, and those you love, with all of your physical needs. Now while your requests are always subject to His will, more often than not, He will deliver. So go ahead and ask Him to bless you. Regardless of outcome, I promise that you'll be glad you did.

With faith, our bodies have extraordinary capabilities... and prayer can literally summon the healing powers of heaven.

Securing Blessings from God Requires Faith

In asking God for blessings, you have to believe that God can answer your prayers. That means you have to demonstrate faith. Just think about the stories in the Bible that highlight this. The woman who touched the hem of Jesus' garment and was healed from a blood disorder; the lame who were given the ability to walk; the blind who were given their sight. Example after example of where people were healed because of their faith.

It's Okay to Ask God to Take This From You

Our prayers took on a whole new meaning when our four-year-old daughter was diagnosed with cancer. To fight this cancer, she went through a year long rigorous regimen of chemotherapy and radiation. Miraculously, at the end of this year, our daughter was cancer-free. We were incredibly relieved and so grateful to God for blessing out family. However, our joy was short-lived.

About two years later, our daughter's cancer returned. Making this news even worse was the doctors telling us that the likelihood of our daughter beating cancer a second time was not very good. Once again, we found ourselves praying and asking our Heavenly Father to help us through this situation.

Around this time, we had a conversation with a friend of ours who said, "Even Christ in the Garden of Gethsemane asked that the cup would pass from Him. But He said, 'Not my will, but yours.'" Our friend went on to say, "It's okay to ask God to take this from you."

To be honest, we had never really asked God to take away our daughter's cancer. We had just been praying to get through everything and be able to deal with whatever God wanted for us. We never really asked for much more than strength. However, after talking to our friend, we now started to ask God to take the cancer from our daughter. We both prayed in a way that we had never prayed before.

The next day, we went to the doctor. Before he was about to proceed with our daughter's treatments, we asked him to check on the status of her cancer. He did some tests and about a half hour later, he came to us and said, "I don't understand this, but there's no cancer there. It's gone."

We went home and told everyone we knew. We were so excited. However, this excitement didn't last long. A little while later, our daughter's oncologist called and said there had been a mistake. The doctor telling us that the cancer was gone had no right to do so. She said more tests needed to be done, but that we shouldn't get our hopes up. She also said that, with all of the scans and tests that had been performed and what she had seen, it just wasn't possible for the cancer to be gone.

About two days later, the oncologist called back and said, "I can't explain it to you. It's completely baffling to me, but there's no cancer there." We knew why. It was because we had asked God.

There was no doubt in our minds that our Heavenly Father healed our little girl and took away her cancer.

Cathy A. - California

In gathering stories for this book, I was privileged to hear and learn about countless examples of how prayers were used to miraculously heal and comfort. This last story was just such an example. Plus, as you've read, on a variety of occasions God has healed me.

Because of my experiences, I know that our prayers really can heal. However, I also know that prayers aren't always answered the way we want. When this happens, it's easy to lose our faith and question the way God works. Although we will discuss unanswered prayers in a future chapter, for now please know that God always does things for the right reasons. He has a plan for each and everyone of us. He loves us and wants us to be happy. Whenever we pray, we must do so with the knowledge that God knows best, and have the faith to accept His will.

4. Having God Bless You With Happiness

Sometimes we get so caught up in the rigors of life that we forget we're supposed to be happy. But that's not what God intended. He didn't put you here to simply grind though life. Instead, He put you here to be happy. But what exactly is happiness and how do you get it?

Happiness Versus Joy

Without downplaying the desire to be happy, I don't think happiness is what we're really after. That's because happiness is a feeling, a by-product of when our circumstances are favorable or positive. But happiness can be fleeting. If our circumstances change, so too can our happiness. So, more than wanting to be happy, I think we more appropriately want to experience joy.

Joy is an attitude or way of thinking that isn't dependent on our circumstances. Sure, we can be happy or sad, depending on what's going on in our life. But, regardless of our situation, we can always have joy. Joy isn't fleeting. It can last forever. With that said, for purposes of our conversation, as we talk about being happy, please know that we're really referring to having joy.

It's funny how God can bless you with the exact thing you ask for, but do it by giving you experiences that you weren't quite expecting.

The Path to Happiness

When I was eighteen years old, I was living in Australia and was trying to figure out what to do with my life. I had finished my first year of university studies and I guess you could say that I didn't feel like my life had much of a purpose.

One particular Sunday, I found myself in church a few minutes earlier than normal. I was thinking about my life and wondering what to do with it. Being overcome with confusion, I put my head down on the pew in front of me and said a silent prayer. I asked God to help me be happy. To help me find a purpose.

As I finished this prayer, I lifted my head and my eyes immediately caught hold of a person whom I had known for many years. I quickly noticed how this person looked extremely happy. In fact, he looked exactly like the way I wanted to feel. I quickly approached him and asked him very bluntly, "Why are you so happy?" Being a few years older than I was, he sensed there was something going on in my life that needed discussing and invited me to talk with him after church.

When church finished, I hurried over to this person and

started talking to him. It was really something how he asked what seemed like just the right questions. It was as though he knew exactly what I was going through. As we spoke, he delicately guided the conversation to a point where he revealed why he was so happy. He said his happiness stemmed from an experience he had several years ago as a church-sponsored missionary. As a missionary, he had the opportunity to live with and help the Aboriginal people of Australia with a variety of their needs. He told me about some of his experiences and how it had given him a deeper perspective on life and what he wanted out of it. Most of all, he emphasized how serving others helped him gain a foundation for happiness.

By the end of this conversation, I was convinced that, if I were to do something similar, I could find the happiness I was looking for. So, like this person had done before me, I decided to become a missionary, and within a few months, I found myself living on the other side of Australia in a small Aboriginal community.

The months I spent with the Aboriginal people were difficult and I faced many challenges. However, as I continued to serve these wonderful people and help them in every possible way that I could, I found myself obtaining the very thing I had prayed for in church that early Sunday morning. I found happiness. In fact, I was happier than I had ever been. All it took was deferring my university studies, traveling across the country, living in an Aboriginal community in the Outback of Australia, and working myself to exhaustion every single day for months on end. Pretty easy, right?

I prayed to be happy and my loving Heavenly Father answered my prayer. As I reflect upon this experience, I think it's wonderful how God can bless you with the exact thing you ask for, but do it by giving you experiences and challenges that you weren't quite expecting.

To this day, my time in the Australian Outback serves as a

reminder of what is most important in life and how, regardless of my situation, I can always find happiness. Most of all, it taught me that true happiness usually comes from serving others as opposed to serving myself.

In your journey along the path of life, don't ever think that you're not supposed to be happy. You are, and God will help you become such. You just need to ask Him. So, if you're in need of a jolt of happiness, you might consider serving others and see how it makes you feel. I guarantee it will quickly change your perspective and make you feel wonderful.

Because of the wonderful and selfless act of the atonement, Jesus made it possible for you to receive a remission of your sins.

Lifting the Burden of Sin

In addition to serving others, oftentimes, the very thing we need in order to be happy is to receive forgiveness for our sins. Fortunately, prayer is a perfect place to ask for this. Because God loves us so very much, He sent His Son to atone for our sins. When you have faith in Jesus and ask God to forgive you, He will.

Just consider the beautiful imagery that Isaiah used when he described how this magnificent process of repentance can eliminate our sins. In Isaiah 1:18 it reads:

> *Though your sins are like scarlet, they shall be as white as snow; though they are red like crimson, they shall become like wool.*

Because of the wonderful and selfless act of the atonement, Jesus made it possible for you to receive a remission of your sins. Speaking from personal experience, I know this is true. I have felt the sweet spirit of the atonement when I have asked God to forgive me of my sins. I know you can feel this, too.

My Path Back to God

My parents taught me about God from a very young age. They took me to church every week and even had me baptized. However, in my early twenties, I stopped going to church and doing the things I had been taught to do. It's not that I stopped believing. It's that I stopped caring.

After about six or seven years of distancing myself from God, things started to change. Or, rather, I started to change. You see, I had come to a point where all I felt was emptiness. Something was missing in my life and no matter how much partying or anything else I did, this emptiness remained. I was tired of living the way I was. I was tired of being miserable, and I needed things to change.

As I thought more about it, I knew what I had to do. I had to start putting God back into my life and following His commandments. I have to admit, because I hadn't been living my life the way I should have, I was nervous about approaching God. I knew I needed Him back in my life, but I was too scared to make the first step. I was embarrassed about all my sins and figured God didn't want to talk to me because of them. Even though I knew God was aware of everything I had done, getting on my knees and telling Him would make everything very real. Part of me felt like it would be easier to just keep living my life the way I was, even though I felt totally empty.

One night, I worked up the courage to offer a prayer. Although it was awkward and I was nervous, I got through it. In fact, I felt pretty good afterward. Enough so that I prayed again the next night and the night after that, too. Then after about two weeks, I got to a point where I felt comfortable asking God to forgive me of my sins and accept me back into His fold. As I said this prayer, I felt a peace and warmth that let me know that because of the sacrifice Jesus had made, God could forgiven me of my sins. I felt so good inside.

As I continued to pray over the next couple months, I was encompassed with God's love again in my life. Gradually, my life wasn't so empty anymore. I was once again experiencing real happiness. I knew God had forgiven me of my sins and my life had a purpose.

Since this time, I've obviously made mistakes, but now I don't wait very long until I ask God to forgive me. I understand that, when I sin, God still loves me. He wants to help me get back on my feet, and He wants to forgive me. If anything, when I'm not doing what is right, that's the time when God wants me to talk to Him the most.

When I think about it now, the truth is that I knew all along that God was the answer, but I tried to convince myself that I didn't need Him to be happy. Now I can't imagine being happy without Him.

Barry J. - Texas

You can have happiness in your life when you listen to what God has to tell you and do what He wants. He knows what will make you truly happy, so go ahead and ask for His help. I promise you that He will give it to you.

When it comes to asking God to help you, there are no limits. Just like my son asked at the baseball game ("Dad, can I get whatever I want?"), you can ask your Heavenly Father to bless you in any possible way and in every single situation.

If you want to be financially independent, God can help you become so. If you want the best relationships imaginable, He can help you to have them. If you or a loved one needs better health, your prayers can be answered and God can heal you and those you love. If you want to experience happiness, God is ready to bestow that upon you. If you're looking for forgiveness, you can get it. With God's help, anything is possible.

Key Principles to Remember

- Just because something seems impossible to you, that doesn't mean it's impossible for God. No matter what you're looking to accomplish, God can help you do it. He can intervene in your life at any time, at any place, and for any reason.

- If one of your goals happens to be financial in nature, getting rich can oftentimes be a by-product of God helping you achieve your goals and reach your full potential.

- God can help make bad relationships good and good relationships better. He can take any relationship, even the most troubled one, and make it fantastic.

- Whatever physically troubles you or those you love, your prayers can summon the healing powers of heaven.

- Much like any loving parent would go to extraordinary lengths to help their children achieve their goals and be happy, your loving Heavenly Father will go to extraordinary lengths to help you achieve your goals and help you be happy.

- Because of the wonderful and selfless act of the atonement, Jesus made it possible for you to receive a remission of your sins.

Chapter Four

What is Prayer?

All I know is that when I pray, coincidences happen;
and when I don't pray, they don't happen.

Dan Hayes

A Conversation Between You and God

By now, I hope you're beginning to understand that developing a better relationship with God through prayer, makes you eligible for some truly incredible blessings. But how do you get to the point where God is willing, perhaps even obliged, to answer your prayers? Well, answering this question begins by defining what prayer actually is. In the next chapter, we'll discuss more about the purpose of prayer.

Prayer is a tool that allows you to communicate with God and provides a way to develop a closer and more personal relationship with Him. In its purest form, prayer is a beautiful and intimate conversation that occurs between a loving Heavenly Father and

His child, you. Best of all, when you pray, you do so directly to God. That's right. Your prayers go directly to God.

As incredible as this is, I'm sad to report that many of us don't appreciate or take advantage of this wonderful privilege as much as we should. For whatever reason, we downplay the fact that we can communicate directly with God and because of this, many of us are cheated out of having the kind of personal relationship with God that is our birthright.

Comforted in My Heart

In early 2002 I worked for Arthur Andersen, the accounting firm whose client was Enron. As a result of the infamous Enron scandal and the corrupt practices of a few people in my firm (of which I wasn't one), all 85,000 worldwide employees in my firm lost their jobs. Never in a million years would I have thought something like that would happen to a company so large and established.

The prospect of losing my job couldn't have come at a worse time. It just so happened that this all took place right at the time when my wife and I were in escrow on the purchase of our first home, and when we were expecting our first child. There I was with those two major obligations and the prospect of no job.

I remember several instances where I pleaded with God to make sure that everything would work out, and that my family would be cared for. I prayed for God's help to know what to do, what decisions to make, and how to pursue getting a new job.

Admittedly, there were a few instances during this time where I was overcome with anxiety. But as I prayed, and I prayed often, without fail I would receive feelings of comfort come into my heart and my mind. I really believe that this was God's way of telling me He loved me, He was keenly aware of my situation, and He was assuring me that everything was going to be okay.

Fortunately, everything turned out to be just like I felt it would. I eventually was able to land a new job, close escrow on my new home and, best of all, welcome my beautiful little girl into the world.

As I look back, I am grateful I was consistent with my prayers before I lost my job. Because I already had a relationship with God I was comfortable asking for His help, and felt entitled to receive it. It wasn't like I came to Him and had to re-introduce myself. I could simply go to Him and get straight to the point of asking for His help, with the full expectation that I would receive it.

I know that when the most unexpected trials or problems occur, having a previously established relationship with God through prayer will help you weather those storms.

Darren W. - California

In order to more fully understand what prayer is and to take full advantage of it, there are four fundamental principles you must understand.

1. *There is No Gatekeeper To God*
2. *Pray in Private*
3. *You Can't Fool God*
4. *Have a Continual Prayer in Your Heart*

God, the most powerful person ever, the ruler of Heaven and Earth, will give you His undivided attention anytime you want.

1. There Is No Gatekeeper to God

One of the most extraordinary things about prayer is that it provides each and every person with a direct link to God. When you initiate contact with God through prayer, it doesn't require getting past a gatekeeper or employing a middleman. You simply don't have to go through anyone to speak with God, not your preacher, pastor, parent, or priest. No one! You can speak with God directly.

Think about that for a moment. God, the most powerful person ever, the ruler of Heaven and Earth, will give you His undivided attention anytime you want. All you have to do is initiate a conversation with Him through prayer. Best of all, when you do pray, God will always be there. You'll never get brushed off because He's too busy. You'll never have to come back at a different time. You'll never get anything less than His full attention.

Whatever You're Doing in Here, Keep Doing It!

When I started the laundry that morning, my little son, Luke, the youngest of six, wanted to watch the clothes spin around in the washing machine. While he was watching the clothes swish back and forth, I heard the back door open. Some of my children had started to go across the street to a convenience store. I quickly left the laundry room to make sure the younger children weren't with them. I then went back downstairs to the laundry area.

To my absolute shock, I saw Luke's feet sticking out of the washing machine. I had totally forgotten about him. I forgot that he was sitting and watching the clothes spin around.

I quickly pulled him out and remember praying aloud to God, "Please help me! Please help me!" Luke wasn't breathing. He was swelling, and he had kind of a bluish-gray color. I laid him there on the floor, and I was somehow able to revive him. He started breathing, but he wasn't conscious. His eyes were still closed. I was so scared.

Meanwhile, my older son had come back from the convenience store. I yelled at him to run to the neighbor's house for help. My neighbor's husband happened to be a fireman. That was the first time I realized that Luke might be burned. I didn't even think about the water being so hot.

My friend called the paramedics and Luke was rushed to the emergency room. Once there, they had me go in a waiting room. I was just constantly praying, of course, just talking to God, "Please watch over him. Please help him." I remember there was a feeling, this peace that just kind of came over me that Luke was going to make it and everything, somehow was going to end up okay.

After a little while, my family and friends had gathered in the waiting room. A doctor told us that Luke probably wouldn't make it past the next forty-five minutes. They were really working hard, trying to figure out what to do for him, but they had lost hope. My husband asked us all to kneel and pray.

In this prayer, my husband's wording placed Luke in the Lord's hands and asked for strength and faith in either case, if he were to live or if he were to die. After we finished the prayer, one of the main doctors came in the waiting room and said, "Well, for some unknown reason, Luke is responding to treatment. Whatever you're doing in here, keep doing it." It was another confirmation that our Heavenly Father knew what was going on and He was in charge. Even though I felt anxiety, I also felt peace. I don't know how those two feelings could be there at the same time, but they were.

Luke remained in intensive care for about four months, and he came close to death several times. During this time, prayer became a way of life. It was the first thing I would think about in the morning, and it was the last thing I'd think about before I went to bed. I was constantly communicating with God because that seemed to be the only way I could figure out how to cope or deal with the situation. Having five other children to think about, prayer was everything to me. It gave me the strength to keep going.

Today, Luke is thirty years old. He is an inspiration to everyone who knows him. He has faced life with so much courage and determination. Even though he has lived with scars over almost his entire body, and things have been difficult, he has never complained. He always tries to be the best he can be. He has a pure testimony of our Lord Jesus Christ and knows that, because of the resurrection, one day his scars will be gone and he will be perfect.

Even though our family has had its share of challenges, I believe these challenges are blessings. They have allowed me to really communicate and get to know God in a way that I never could have. My family has been blessed so much because of what has happened.

Pam J. - Colorado

As your loving Father, God didn't create you to then abandon you or give you anything less than what He is capable of giving. Rather, He put you here with the full expectation that your relationship with Him would thrive, and He gave you the ability to do this through the magnificent process of prayer.

2. *Pray in Private*

I remember a man, who attended the same church as me in my hometown of Australia. This man was notorious for calling attention to himself and everything he did. No gift he gave went unacknowledged (by him). No good deed he did went unheralded (by him). No lofty thought he presented wasn't highlighted (by him). This guy seemed to be more concerned with the praise he received from others than actually helping someone in need or doing something worthwhile.

In contrast to this, I recently read about a couple here in the United States who, by all outward appearances, seemed to live a very humble life. When this man and his wife passed away, it was learned that, during the course of their lives, they had donated over $10 million to charity. This was a complete surprise to everyone who knew them. Even the couple's children were unaware of their parents' wealth and subsequent philanthropic activities.

I share these contrasting stories with you to highlight that, when you do things, you can do them in one of two ways: either privately and for no one to see, or in public so everyone might see and recognize what you're doing. With that said, when it comes to prayer, it is best done in private. It is meant to be intimate and personal, a one-on-one conversation with you and God. It's not something you do for the praise of others or to show off. Granted, there are times when it's appropriate to pray in public, such as in church or when you're leading group prayer, but developing a more perfect relationship with God comes primarily from praying in private. Matthew 6:5–6 sums it up most adeptly.

> *And when you pray, you must not be like the hypocrites. For they love to stand and pray in the synagogues and at the street corners, that they may be seen by others. Truly, I say to you, they have received their reward.*
>
> *But when you pray, go into your room and shut the door and pray to your Father who is in secret. And your Father who sees in secret will reward you.*

Doesn't this passage just say it all? I particularly love the promise that Jesus offers, that if you pray in secret, God will reward you. I'll bet the couple I mentioned previously, the ones who gave so much, felt overwhelmed at the extent to which God rewarded or blessed them. They weren't concerned about advertising their generosity and receiving the praise of others. They simply wanted to do their part, and it seems as though God certainly blessed them for it.

On the other hand, the man from Australia who attended the same church as me, probably didn't enjoy a similar bounty from God. I guess you could say that he had figured out how to achieve his reward on Earth, that being, receiving the praise of others. Given the choice, I'll take being blessed by God over the praise of man any day. What about you?

My Dad's Example

When my siblings and I were growing up, my father never really did the church thing. He left that up to my mom. Every Sunday, my mom would take us kids to church, and that's how it was. Now, even though my dad didn't go to church, I knew he believed in God. I especially knew that he believed in prayer. Every morning before he left for work, he would get all of the family together, and we would kneel down and pray. At night, he would take each of us kids to our beds and have us kneel down with him and say our prayers. In addition to this, I would often walk into my dad's room and find him kneeling beside his bed, praying by himself.

I can't tell you how powerful an impression this had on my mind. I knew that prayer was important to my dad, and this helped make prayer important to me too.

Now that I am a father, I have adopted a similar practice of praying with my family before I leave for work and before they go to sleep at night. I have tried to be consistent with my personal prayers too. Doing this has brought me closer to God. Better yet, it has bought my family closer together. Just like it did when I was a kid.

Paul G. - California

Why You Need to Pray in Private

For God to bless you, you have to develop a personal relationship with Him. You have to come to know Him, and you can't do this if you're not talking to Him privately. Think about the relationships you have with your spouse, your children, and some of your very best friends. How much time have you spent with these people, particularly one-on-one time? Think of your efforts to get to know these people, talking with them, interacting with them, and loving them. Now ask yourself, "Why would it be any different with God?" It wouldn't. It's not! Getting to know God takes being with God and this happens most effectively when you pray to Him in a one-on-one manner. It happens when you pray to Him in private.

Fulfilling Your Dreams

God is the ultimate power, and He can intervene in your life for any reason. However, if you remember from earlier, you have to actually ask God for the things you most want, and this probably isn't happening if you're not praying in secret. You see, when you're alone with God, you can share your most intimate thoughts and your most outlandish dreams. You can dream big and then dream a little bigger. Plus, prayer is a secure place. It's where God will listen to you without judgment or skepticism.

When you in private you can be yourself and share with God the things you simply aren't comfortable sharing with others. Better yet, you get to share these things with an all-powerful Father who can do anything. Upon listening to your requests, He can make things happen that otherwise wouldn't.

Above all, praying in private demonstrates your humility. It lets God know that you're less concerned about the praise of others and more concerned about developing a better relationship with Him.

When you go to God in prayer, be yourself. That's the only way you can hope to develop a perfect relationship with Him.

3. *You Can't Fool God, So Don't Even Try*

Because God knows you (and every little intimate thing about you), coming to Him in prayer is about being yourself. You don't have to pretend to be someone you're not. You don't have to work on having an impressive vocabulary or figure out persuasive arguments to put before Him. It just doesn't need to be that way. Besides, God already knows everything about you, it's not like you're going to fool Him. In fact, if you try to be someone you're not, it can actually prevent you from developing the kind of relationship with God that will encourage Him to bless you. Let me give you an example.

In college, I had a crush on a particular girl. She was pretty and smart, and I really liked her. The only problem was that when I was around her, I became a different person. I felt like I was always trying to impress her and make her think I was better than I really was. In fact, it got to the point where being with her was more nerve-wracking than enjoyable. Yes, I was smitten and at the time, I thought I wanted things to progress. However, trying to be a different person was taking its toll. It wasn't long before she dumped me and in hindsight, thank goodness she did. Although I didn't know it at the time, she wasn't right for me. I had to fool her into thinking I was someone that I wasn't. That's not a relationship that can ever work, and it's not a relationship that would allow either party to truly know one another.

It's the same with God. You can't expect to know God if you approach Him under false pretenses. Like any relationship, if it's built on a lie, it cannot become perfect. So, when you go to God in prayer, you must be yourself, and you must be completely honest. That's the only way you can hope to develop a perfect relationship with Him, one that will warrant His blessings.

MY AMAZING TRANSFORMATION

From as early as I can remember, I spoke with a stutter. In high school I was teased a lot, and had very few friends. On the bright side, not having many friends allowed me to study a lot and I was accepted into a great school for college.

Now as excited as I was to be going to college, I feared my experience would be similar to that of high school, and when I thought about it from this perspective, my excitement quickly subsided. I wanted my stutter gone, but I had tried so many things in the past to help me, and nothing had worked. I felt like there was nothing I could do.

Around this time, I remember attending a Christian youth convention where a speaker talked about how God could perform miracles. As he was talking I felt a peace about his words and believed that this was God's way of telling me that I could be healed of my stutter.

That night, I prayed and begged God to help me. I told Him that I couldn't figure out why I stuttered and I really needed His help. That I needed a miracle. Now although I had prayed many times about this in the past, this prayer was different. I had such a greater sense of urgency and intensity. As I continued to pray, I felt very optimistic that everything was going to be okay.

As the summer months between my final year of high school and my first year of college passed, I continued to pray for my stutter to disappear, but I wasn't seeing any progress. Finally, when it came time to go to college, I must admit that I was disappointed that my stutter was still with me, and I was fearful of what was ahead.

Sure enough, in one of my very first classes, the professor asked me a question, and in an attempt to answer it, I was a mess. It was so bad that I didn't even get through my sentence before the professor politely interrupted me and went on with his lecture. To make matters worse, a few people in the class laughed when I was trying to speak. I can't describe how embarrassed I felt. My eyes welled up with tears, and I so wished I could have disappeared.

Then something remarkable happened. At the end of the class, about a half-dozen people came up to me and introduced themselves. They commented on how bad they felt that others had laughed and they said that I was very courageous. I thanked them for their words and left feeling a little better about what had just happened.

Later that week, I saw a few of the people from this class, and they extended the same degree of friendship and kindness outside of class as they did the first time I met them. In fact, I went on to become good friends with a few of them. I can't tell you what this did for my self-esteem.

After a little while of enjoying my new friendships and continuing to pray, I noticed my speech was getting better. I was able to say the words that my mind was thinking. Miraculously, my stutter was starting to disappear. I was even starting to volunteer answers in my classes. That's something I had never done before.

Slowly but surely, things got better. I worked closely with a speech therapist, and there were days at a time where I didn't stutter at all.

Today, I am virtually stutter-free. I have many close friends, a wonderful family, and a level of confidence that I never thought was possible for someone like me. On occasion, I even teach seminars to Christian youth groups about how God can help you overcome adversity. Talk about coming full circle.

My prayers weren't answered overnight, but they were answered. I know that God somehow did something for me to help my stutter. Perhaps

He just put the right kind of people in my life to be my friends, or perhaps it was a literal physical change. I don't know. What I do know is that He answered my prayers and helped me out in a way that I needed most.

Derek K. - Minnesota

4. Have a Continual Prayer in Your Heart

In the Scriptures, we often read that we must "pray always." But what does this mean? For me, I believe that I am "praying always" in two ways.

First, I like to pray formally at least twice a day. Once in the morning, and again before going to sleep. My morning prayer helps my mind dwell more on God throughout the day. My evening prayer serves as an extension of my morning prayer, comforting me as I go to sleep and preparing me for the following day.

When I arise the next day, I once again begin with a prayer. When it comes time to retire for the evening, per my practice, I pray again. This pattern continues every day and eventually becomes a cycle of continuous prayer. It's easy to see how praying like this, day after day and year after year, might be what the Scriptures refer to as "praying always."

Second, I like to pray in my heart. You see, my personal conversations with God aren't limited to my formal prayers. Nor should yours be limited in this way either. You can talk to God at any time and in any place. You don't need to be on your knees, and you don't need to go through the traditional steps of prayer. You can talk to God in your mind and your heart. You can have a running dialogue with God at all times. I believe this also constitutes "praying always."

If we are persistent in calling upon God, or "praying always," we are more likely to get what we want.

Your Persistence Will be Rewarded

The Scriptures tell us that, if we are persistent in calling upon God, or if we are "praying always," we are more likely to get what we want. For example, in Luke 11, Jesus shares the parable about the man who went to a friend's house at midnight and began knocking on the door. This man needed three loaves of bread, but the friend inside says the door is locked for the night and to go away.

> *I tell you, though he will not get up and give him anything because he is his friend, yet because of his impudence he will rise and give him whatever he needs.*
>
> *And I tell you, ask, and it will be given to you; seek, and you will find; knock, and it will be opened to you.*
>
> (Luke 11:8–9)

In this Scripture, Jesus tells us that the persistence of the man knocking on the door was eventually rewarded. His friend was obliged to get up and give him what he wanted. Not because of their friendship, but because he just didn't want to be bothered anymore. Likewise, your prayers can be answered because of your persistence. Not that God is going to cave into your requests, or that He wants you to go away and stop annoying Him. Rather, God simply likes it when you're persistent with your prayers. He likes it when you "pray always."

So once again, what is prayer? It is a beautiful and intimate conversation that occurs between a loving Heavenly Father and His child, you. It is a tool that allows you to communicate and come closer to God. It will allow God to instruct you, warn you, and, of course, bless you.

Key Principles to Remember

- Prayer is a tool that allows you to communicate with God and develop a closer and more personal relationship with Him.
- You don't have to go through anyone to speak with God. You can speak with God directly.
- Getting to know God takes being with God and this happens when you pray to Him in private.
- You can't fool God! When you go to Him in prayer, you must be yourself, and you must be completely honest.
- You can pray at any time by talking to God in your mind and your heart.
- God rewards persistence. He likes it when you "pray always."

Chapter Five

Getting Comfortable With Prayer

Satan does not care how many people read about prayer if only he can keep them from praying.

Paul E. Billheimer

Empty Phrases

Growing up, it seemed like my parents asked me every night before I fell asleep if I had said my prayers. While I certainly didn't object to them asking, in hindsight, I'm not sure if the prayers I offered were all that sincere. Although I would thank God for my family, and ask Him to help me in school, sports, or whatever was on my mind at the time, I don't remember my prayers lasting for more than a couple minutes, and they certainly didn't vary much from night to night. To be completely honest, I'm not sure if these prayers were said to develop a better relationship with God, as opposed to just checking something off my to-do list.

Unfortunately, our prayers are often like this. Rather than trying to develop a more perfect relationship with God, we say our prayers out of obligation. In doing so, we tend to say the exact same thing every time we speak with God. Our prayers are nothing more than what the Scriptures refer to as "empty phrases."

> *And when you pray, do not heap up empty phrases as the Gentiles do, for they think that they will be heard for their many words.*
>
> (Matthew 6:7)

Just imagine if every time you saw a particular person, you said the exact same thing. Do you think that person would think you're a little strange? I'm sure they would and I can't see how your relationship with them would be anything but casual at best. Sadly, though, that's how many of us talk with God when we pray. Yes, we approach Him on a daily basis and this is certainly a good thing, but, all too often, we say the exact same thing, day after day after day.

Now, don't get me wrong. I'm not saying you shouldn't be praying for the same things every day or you shouldn't recite the Lord's Prayer if you feel so inclined. What I am saying is when you do speak with God, your words need to be more than just a set of memorized lines. They need to have feeling, and they need to convey your sincerity. Otherwise, you'll never be able to develop the kind of relationship with God that is requisite for Him to bless you in the way we've been talking about.

After praying with a little more intensity just one time, I was closer to God.

Getting Comfortable with Prayer

So, how can you make the transition from saying the "empty phrases" kind of prayers that Jesus warned us against, to saying the kind of prayers that will allow you to develop a better and more meaningful relationship with God? Better yet, how do you get comfortable with saying prayers period? Well, let me tell you how I did it.

Many years ago, I realized that my relationship with God needed improving, and that my prayers needed to be more sincere. So one night, I decided to experiment with my prayers. Instead of just reciting what I normally did, which usually only took about three or four minutes, I decided to set a time limit for my prayer. That night, I was going to pray for at least fifteen minutes. I figured that doing so would be an initial step in helping me improve my relationship with God.

I got on my knees, rested up against my bed, and started praying. Now keep in mind I was convinced that this prayer was going to be the start of my new and improved relationship with God. I was ready for something magical to happen and was eager to get started. I began my prayer and after covering the things I normally prayed for, I peeked at the clock in my bedroom. To my absolute shock, I hadn't even hit the three-minute mark and I was out of things to say. What was I going to pray about for the remaining time? How was this prayer going to change my life?

Sadly, I still didn't know how to really pray. What I thought had been good and meaningful prayers were nothing more than slightly revised versions of the prayers that I had said as a child. Without realizing it, I was saying the "empty phrases" kind of prayers that weren't going to help me develop the kind of relationship with God that I wanted. Sure, I was asking God to bless me and take care of my family, but I wasn't doing it with the sincerity, intensity, or gratitude that I should have been.

After coming to the stark realization that my prayers were totally inadequate, and without knowing what else to say, I figured I'd just talk to God, like I would my parents or someone I really cared for. So that's what I did. I shared with God what I was thinking and feeling, the needs of my children, the goals of my family, and what I wanted to accomplish. I talked about everything I could think of. As I spoke, which was more of an inner dialogue, more and more poured out of me, and I had a very personal, in-depth conversation with God. I looked at my clock again and I couldn't believe it. My fifteen minutes were up. And I was just getting started!

Even though this prayer was at first somewhat awkward and I stumbled through parts of it, afterward, I distinctly remember feeling closer to God. How about that! After praying with a little more intensity and for a longer duration just one time, I was closer to God. I immediately thought to myself, "If I feel this good and this close to God after praying like this just once, imagine how much closer I'll feel toward God if I pray this way every night!" Certainly, I would accomplish my goal of developing a more intimate and rewarding relationship with God.

From that point on, night after night, I got on my knees and prayed for at least fifteen minutes. This was sometimes relatively easy to do; other times, it wasn't. But in spite of the occasional difficulty, I put a great deal of effort into my prayers and I was very determined to make them work. My language was casual, but reverent. I told God everything I could think of, and I tried to be myself. And that's when it happened.

Slowly but surely, I developed a more intimate and more personal relationship with God. A kinship so extraordinarily close that every time I spoke with God, I felt like He was not only listening, but also answering. And that's exactly what I had hoped for.

Developing this more personal relationship with God required a considerable effort on my part, but the payoff was worth it. I had become completely comfortable with prayer, and I was at total ease with God. Yes, it took a little while, but, over time, my prayers got better. They became truly heartfelt. My relationship with God improved, and it was on the path to becoming perfect. Best of all, my efforts allowed me to come to a better understanding and appreciation of the fact that God is my Father and I am His child.

The Burden Was Gone

We were really excited to be having our second child and at our twenty-week ultrasound, we were looking forward to finding out if we were having a boy or a girl. To share in this excitement, we decided to bring our two-year-old daughter so she could see her baby brother or sister.

As I lay on the table, I started to feel like something might be wrong even before the ultrasound had started. I just thought I was being a little too worrisome. However, my fears were realized, and we found out that our unborn baby had Trisomy 13.

The ultrasound technician told us our baby would not live long and an abortion might be a good option, but we truly believed that was Heavenly Father's decision to make, not ours. I then asked if it were a boy or a girl. When I found out she was a girl, I named her Aubrielle. My husband and I said we would love her no matter what. She was special and a big part of our family.

Even though I cried a lot that night, I knew I had a decision to make. I could be sad and depressed and feel sorry for myself, or I could count my blessings and look to the positive side of my pregnancy. I started to think about all the people who were in a worse situation than I was. There are mothers in the world who cannot feed their children and have to constantly worry about their safety. I also know women who could not get pregnant. I felt so blessed to be pregnant with Aubrielle, and to have such good doctors to help me.

As time passed, we prepared ourselves for everything. We knew our daughter might be stillborn or might not breathe once she was born. Even if she did breathe, she probably wouldn't live for more than a few hours.

The night before I was scheduled to have Aubrielle, I was taking a shower, and tears started to stream down my face. I could not control them. I felt as if I were getting ready to go to my own death. The pain was so great, and I knew I could not bear it on my own. I asked my Heavenly Father to help me and comfort me. Not even a second had passed when the burden I was carrying was gone. I understood that what was going to happen was meant to be and my Heavenly Father was there to help me through it. I was not alone, and Aubrielle would be okay. Because of this prayer, I felt the happiness and comfort that I so desperately needed and was prepared for the next day.

Miraculously, Aubrielle was born alive and we were so excited to hold her. I remember seeing her in my husband's arms and being consumed with love. Even with her cleft lip and palate, she was perfect and gorgeous. She was so beautiful. I cannot put into words how much love I felt for her. When my two-year-old daughter held her little sister and sang to her, it felt like the whole world stopped for a few minutes. I cannot describe how wonderful it was. I wish everyone could have been there to experience it. I felt so lucky to have the two of them as my daughters. I felt so much gratitude to my Heavenly Father for my family.

Aubrielle went on to live for four more hours and then peacefully passed away. I would not trade those four hours for anything. It was worth all the physical pain. If I had to go through it all over again with my next pregnancy, it would be worth it.

Having experienced the peace the night before I had Aubrielle helped bring me comfort when she passed away. I knew she was with a loving and caring Father who loves her as much as He loves me.

As I look back, I think that in order to receive this comfort from our Heavenly Father, like I did, we need to be willing to let go of anger and fear and just invite Him into our hearts. We have to be willing to let Him comfort us. It is the only reason I was okay. If I did not have that comfort from my Heavenly Father, the death of my daughter would have destroyed me.

I am so lucky to have had Aubrielle, and I know I will be with her again one day. She is a perfect, special angel. I learned so much from a little girl who never said a word to me. I am the luckiest person in the world to have her as my daughter. Every time I think about her, she brings me such happiness. I am so proud of her, and I am proud to be her mom. She was worth it all.

Holly R. - California

You too can become comfortable with prayer and develop a more meaningful relationship with God, but it will take practice and effort. However don't be discouraged if at first this seems hard. You can do this!

Committing to the Prayer Process

As you go about trying to get more comfortable with prayer, perhaps you can do what I did. Make a goal of setting aside a specific amount of time each day to simply talk with God. Maybe it's ten or fifteen minutes, or perhaps it's less. Regardless, commit to talking with God on a daily basis and go beyond what you're currently comfortable with. At first, this may be challenging, but I assure you that, as you commit to this, your bond with God will quickly grow, and your prayer life, as well as your regular life, will become more and more incredible.

When you pray, speak with God about everything you can think of. Share with Him all of your goals and dreams, your frustrations, and victories. Allow Him to become your best friend and most trusted confidante. Acknowledge your shortcomings, and ask for His understanding and forgiveness. Above all, approach Him in complete sincerity and honesty. Be yourself, and don't be afraid to ask for His help in getting to know Him.

If you do this, your closeness to God will get to a point where you'll feel comfortable asking God to bless you with all the things you're looking for... no matter how trivial or earth-shaking. That's exactly the kind of relationship I think Jesus knew you'd need when He said,

> *And whatever you ask in prayer, you will receive, if you have faith.*
>
> (Matt 21:22)

The Why of Prayer

Like many children, my children, often ask "Why?" Why do I have to do this? Why should I do that? If you've ever been around children, or have children of your own, you can probably relate.

Now, sometimes, unless I explain to my children the why of a situation, they don't always do what I ask, and as a parent, this can be rather frustrating. While I don't ever want to squash their inquisitiveness, I sometimes wish they would just do, instead of always having to ask why.

I share this because we are often like this with God. We need to know the "why," before we actually go ahead and "do." It's therefore important to discuss the four whys of prayer.

1. *To Develop a Relationship With God*
2. *To Demonstrate Gratitude to God*
3. *To Ask God to Bless You and Others*
4. *To Receive Instruction From God*

While praying and asking God to bless you is totally acceptable, it's not the primary purpose of prayer.

1. *Developing a Relationship With God*

Although we have talked about how prayer is designed to help you develop a better relationship with God, it's important to discuss this in a little more detail. In doing this, I'd like to tell you about a friend of mine. This friend calls me every now and again to catch up, or at least that's what he thinks he's doing. In truth, he really calls only when he needs something, and he uses the pretense of catching up as a way of asking me for a favor. Let me assure you, when he does this, it's very transparent and somewhat insulting. Perhaps you have a friend like this too. Perhaps it's even a member of your family.

I share this brief anecdote because I want you to ask yourself two very important questions. First, do you approach God to really catch up, or, like my friend, do you go to Him only when you need something? Second, even if you do pray regularly, do your prayers focus solely on asking God for favors?

If you answered yes to either of these questions, then there's work to be done. You see, while praying and asking God to bless you is totally acceptable, it's not the primary purpose of prayer.

That's because the primary purpose of prayer is to develop a better relationship with God. Remember, God didn't put you here to ignore you or be an absentee father. Rather, He put you here with the full expectation that your relationship with Him would thrive, and He appointed prayer as the divine means to do this.

OKAY, GOD, HERE'S YOUR CHANCE

One night, I was out having a good time with some friends and, at one point during the evening, I remember walking out of the rest room and catching a glimpse of myself in the mirror. I stopped and started staring at myself. I was alone and something about the way I looked made me question who I had become. I started asking myself all kinds of questions. "What are you doing? What have you become? Is this what God wants you to do? Is this what you want to do?" I had this feeling that I needed to make a change in my life, but I didn't know what that was or where to start.

The next morning, the thought came to my mind that I needed to move across country to live with my father on the West Coast. Now as silly as it sounds, I took a quarter and said, "Heads, I stay. Tails, I go." I flipped the coin and it came up tails.

Not entirely convinced I said, "Okay, I'll do two out of three." So I flipped the quarter again. Again it came up tails. Now even though this should have cemented my decision to move, I was a little reluctant to let a coin toss decide my fate. So I grabbed the quarter, clenched it in my fist, held it to my heart and said, "Okay, God, here's your chance. If you want me to go and live with my father, here's your chance to tell me." All of a sudden, I felt this amazing peace throughout my body and I knew that it was God telling me that I should move to be with my dad.

When I moved to live with my father, I enrolled in school. I didn't know anyone and didn't have any friends. They were all back home. I thought, "Okay, God, I did what you told me to do. I moved out here. Now what?"

That's when my prayers became everything to me. I found myself praying all the time. In the morning when I woke up. At night before I went to sleep. During the day while I was driving. Every chance I could, I spoke with God, and my relationship with Him grew so much because of this. God became an enormous part of my life. So, even though at times I felt alone, it was comforting to know that I really wasn't alone.

Today, I am married, have a wonderful family, and many close friends. Best of all, when I look in the mirror, I like what I see. I like the path that I'm on and believe I'm doing what God wants me to do. Every now and again, I picture Him looking at me as well, and saying, "Good job, son. You're doing great, and I love you."

Brandon W. - Nevada

2. Demonstrating Gratitude to God

Do you remember the parable of the ten lepers? It's where Jesus healed ten people suffering from leprosy, and only one of them returns to say thank you.

> *Then one of them, when he saw that he was healed, turned back, praising God with a loud voice;*
>
> *And he fell on his face at Jesus' feet, giving him thanks. Now he was a Samaritan.*
>
> *Then Jesus answered, "Were not ten cleansed? Where are the nine?*
>
> *Was no one found to return and give praise to God except this foreigner?"*
>
> (Luke 17:15–18)

I love the way this parable seems to elicit the same question from almost everyone who reads it. How could these people be so ungrateful? And while they certainly were ungrateful, I think there's a bigger point that Jesus was trying to make here. Yes, it's easy to recognize when others are being ungrateful, but is it as easy to recognize when you're being individually ungrateful? Particularly to God? I'm not sure it is. Think about your own life. How often do you thank God for your health or the health of your loved ones? What about your job or your home? What about the fact that you can read this book or the thousands of other things that God has blessed you with?

In truth, everything you have is a result of God giving it to you. Freedom, education, health, safety, love, happiness, family, hope, knowledge that Jesus is our Savior. It's imperative that you continually thank God for all of your blessings. Fortunately, prayer is the perfect place to do this.

Recognizing Your Dependence on God

Being grateful for all of your blessings allows you to more readily acknowledge your total dependence on God. Plus, it helps you become a better person. You see, when you come to appreciate that everything you have in this life is from God, your love for God will naturally increase. When this happens you'll more likely follow His commandments.

Mom, I Made a New Friend

I looked at all the other moms and noticed many of them were fighting back tears. I thought to myself, "Should I feel bad about not being sad? After all, it is my daughter's first day of school." Grace was starting the first grade and for the first time, she would be at school for a full day. Instead of being sad, I was imagining how peaceful the next six hours were going to be.

Just as I had hoped, my day was peaceful and quiet. I accomplished so many things that were just not possible to do with all of my kids. However, my "me time" was over, and it was time to pick up the kids from school.

My son made his way quickly to where we were to meet, outside of Grace's classroom. As we were waiting for her class to be dismissed, I was talking with a few of the parents. One of them mentioned that there was a blind girl in the class who was new to our school. We all wondered how this would affect the class and hoped that it would be a very positive thing for our kids. We hoped that this little girl would be well accepted and treated kindly. The students then began filing out of the classroom, grabbing their backpacks and reuniting with their parents. There was no sign of Grace. I expected to see her coming out with her friends, excited to tell me about her first day.

There was a lot of commotion as all of the kids left the classroom. A few minutes had passed, and still no Grace. I was just about to go and peek my head in the classroom when I saw her. She was coming out the door and she wasn't alone. It turns out that she had stayed after class to help this girl, who we had just been talking about. Grace was walking side by side with the little blind girl, their arms locked together. I watched, as she tenderly guided her through the door and carefully led her to her mother. I will never forget the sweet, caring expression on my daughter's face. Seeing my six-year-old help this little blind girl walk to her mom was one of the most beautiful and touching things I had ever seen. My eyes began to well up.

I never thought that I would be one of those moms who cried on the first day of school, but I just couldn't help it. My daughter's kindness and love struck me. It was so sweet! After walking the little girl to her mom, my daughter came up to me and whispered, "Mom, I made a new friend, and she's blind!" I embraced my daughter and felt such a sense of gratitude for this beautiful experience.

Taryn B. - California

The next time you pray, begin your prayer by thinking about everything you've been blessed with. Pour out your soul in thanks to God, and be as exhaustive as you can. If you do this, it won't take long before you'll start to feel an overwhelming sense of love toward God and all that He has done for you.

3. Asking God to Bless You

Once you have finished thanking God for all you have, you can begin to ask Him to bless you and those you love. To me, this is really exciting because your prayers give you the opportunity to ask God to bless you in any manner that you want. And, like we've mentioned, because God can do anything, He can answer any prayer. He can help you achieve all of your goals and dreams. No matter what they are.

Asking God to bless you further highlights just how much we all depend on Him. Allow me to explain.

Perhaps like you, I have realized that so many things in life are out of my control. I can't always protect my family. I can't control the actions of others, and I can't control what's going to happen. But there is something I can control. I can control the sincerity, intensity, and content of my prayers.

With this in mind, on a daily basis, I ask God to bless me and those I love. I ask for safety, good health, help overcoming challenges and trials, help with my business, help to be a better father and husband, a better person, and so much more. Truth be told, I ask for so many things that I simply couldn't get through life without God's assistance. And you know what? Neither can you.

If you take the challenge to pray for at least ten to fifteen minutes a day, you're going to have lots of time to communicate with God, so take some of that time and ask God to bless you and those you love.

4. *Receiving Instruction From God*

The final purpose of prayer is to receive instruction from God. This is where God can actually guide and influence your actions, thoughts, and deeds, and provide you with answers to your questions.

Because of His divine foresight, God knows the consequences of your actions and the actions of others, and He can use this knowledge to help bless your life and those you love.

God Can Answer Your Questions

God, the most powerful, most knowledgeable, and most loving person ever, can answer your individual questions, guide your decisions and influence your actions. Best of all, when God does this, it's from a standpoint of wanting to make your life the best it can be. His counsel will always be for your personal benefit, growth, and protection.

Just think of what Jesus said about the person who listens to the counsel of God. He comes out ahead.

> *Everyone then who hears these words of mine and does them will be like a wise man who built his house on the rock.*
>
> *And the rain fell, and the floods came, and the winds blew and beat on that house, but it did not fall, because it had been founded on the rock.*
>
> (Matt 7:24–25)

God Can Bless, Guide, and Warn You

Because of His divine foresight, God can bless you, guide you, and even warn you. He knows the consequences of your actions and the actions of others, and He can use this knowledge to help bless your life and those you love. Just think of the countless Biblical examples of where God has done this. When He warned Mary and Joseph to flee into Egypt to protect Jesus. Where He guided the three wise men to the infant Jesus. When He instructed Noah on how to build an ark. When He revealed to Pharaoh to store grain so he and his kingdom might survive the approaching famine. Time and time again, God has guided, blessed, and even warned His people, and He can do the same for you.

I Just Had a Feeling

When I was about fifteen years old, I came home from school one afternoon and got ready to do my homework. As I sat down, I had an overwhelming feeling to get up and look for my older brother. I didn't understand why I was getting this feeling, but it was so strong that I couldn't ignore it.

I started looking in and around the house, but I couldn't find him anywhere. Then I had the inclination to get on my bicycle and ride around my neighborhood in the hope I might see him. To be honest, I didn't have any idea where I was going, but I kept riding because the feeling I was having was too powerful to allow me to stop.

After about fifteen minutes, I found myself at the local park and saw my brother lying down in the middle of a field. I rode my bike up to him and asked if everything was all right. As I looked at him, I knew something was wrong, but I didn't know what. After a little bit of small talk, I said, "Let's go home." He agreed, and we made our way back. We didn't really say much along the way, but, when we arrived home, I felt at peace and didn't feel the need to press him as to what was going on.

Many years later, I was talking with my mother one night and she asked if I remembered the experience. Yes, I remembered, and had often wondered what it all meant. My mother went on to tell me that, on that particular day, my brother was in a complete state of depression, and was contemplating all kinds of crazy things. She said, "Your brother told me that, if you hadn't shown up that day, we might have never seen him again."

I am convinced that God was talking directly to my soul that day and He was instructing me to find my brother. I am so glad that God loves me and my family so much that He will warn us in times of uncertainty and danger. I'm especially glad that I listened.

Tyler N. - Ohio

Whether you ask God to keep your family safe, help your business prosper, be completely happy, or simply help you make good decisions, He can give you the help and guidance you need to bless your life. In the coming chapter, I'll discuss in more detail just exactly how He does this.

Getting to know God and developing a better relationship with Him can transform you into a better, happier, and more successful person. When you are close with God, you naturally start looking at life from a different perspective. You start to see things the way

God sees them and this, in turn, allows Him to influence more of your decisions and actions.

When you're close to God and you put your trust in Him, He can guide and influence your life in a way that is best for you. He can transform your life, making it so much better than it otherwise would be. You simply need to commit to praying with more energy and intensity. Step out of your prayer comfort zone and challenge yourself to get to truly know God. As you do, I know you will be blessed, and your relationship with God will blossom. I know because it happened for me, and it can happen for you, too.

Key Principles to Remember

- When you speak with God, your words need to be more than just a set of memorized lines. They need to have feeling, and they need to convey sincerity.

- To develop a better relationship with God, commit to praying on a daily basis and go beyond what you're currently comfortable with.

- There are four main purposes of prayer:

  1. **To develop a relationship with God-** God put you here with the full expectation that your relationship with Him would thrive.
  2. **To demonstrate gratitude to God-** Everything you have is a result of God giving it to you, and it's imperative that you continually thank Him for this.
  3. **To ask God to bless you and others-** Prayer is the perfect place to ask God to bless your life and those you love.
  4. **To receive instruction from God-** God can guide and influence your actions, thoughts, and deeds, and can provide you with answers to your questions.

Chapter Six

How God Answers Prayers

God does not send thunder if a still, small voice is enough.

Neal Maxwell

If You Really Want Something, Pray about It

When I was about ten years old, I had an experience with prayer that still ranks as one of my favorites. One morning, I told my mother how I wished I could be in a race for the school athletics carnival that day. However, because the kids in the race had already been chosen, I wasn't going to be able to participate. Within a second, she said, "Well, if you really want something, you should just pray about it."

Although I had been taught about prayer and knew it was something you could do to ask for God's help on things, I had never really considered what that meant. After all, I was only ten years old. But, when my mother suggested I pray about being in the race that day, it was a light bulb moment. I realized I could use prayer as a tool to help me with the things I wanted. Upon coming to this realization, I got really excited.

Armed with this knowledge, I went into my room, got down on my knees, folded my arms, and offered a very simple prayer asking God to let me participate in the race that day. After that, I got up and went to school with the full expectation that God would answer my prayer.

When I got to school, I made my way down to the athletics field. After watching a few of the younger children run in their races, the starting official called the names of the children who were running in "my" race to the starting line. He told them to take their marks. They followed these instructions by crouching over the starting line, eagerly waiting for the gun to go off. Meanwhile, I stood on the sidelines, waiting for God to answer my prayer.

Despite the fact that the race was literally seconds from starting and I had not yet been asked to participate, I still believed I would run in this race. After all, I had prayed and asked God to make this happen and I truly believed that it would.

Then, with starting gun in hand, the race official (who happened to be my teacher) came over to me, grabbed me forcefully, and said, "Bentley, I want you in this race. Get in there!" I did what he ordered and within seconds, the race began with me in it. God answered my prayer! Looking back, perhaps I should have asked God to help me win the race because as it turned out, I finished in second-to-last place.

As I think about this experience, I feel so blessed to have witnessed the amazing power of prayer at such a young age. Even as a ten-year-old boy, I knew I had something that many other kids my age didn't: the knowledge that prayer really worked. Even today, as I reflect upon this experience, it inspires me. It reminds me that when we have faith, God can answer any prayer.

A Crash Course in Prayer

It was 1964. I was just a young boy and as a family, we had all been to Chicago to attend my uncle's wedding. As we took off for home from the airport, we all heard this big "thud." I wondered what it was, but, because no one seemed to be worrying about it, I didn't worry either.

About an hour before landing, the captain of the plane informed everyone that the landing gear was not working. That big "thud" was something after all, and the crew was now preparing for an emergency landing. I was sitting next to my mother, and she started to cry. In fact, all around me, people were crying, and I was very scared.

I remembered having been taught about prayer and figured that saying a prayer would be a good idea. I bowed my head and offered a very simple prayer. Although I can't remember what I said, I remember the feeling I had. It was this sense of peace and comfort. I knew that everything was going to be all right. Although I didn't know it at the time, I now recognize that I was feeling the Holy Ghost.

I looked at my mom. "Mom, we're going to be okay."

"How do you know?"

"Because I prayed."

She then looked as though she had been reminded of something she had forgotten. She wiped her eyes, and then she prayed as well.

Even though everyone else was in a panic, we were both calm.

Although it was very rough, we landed safely. We were all right!

Everyone cheered for the captain of the plane, but I was cheering for Heavenly Father. I knew He had answered my prayer and allowed us to land safely.

Marc A. - California

The Different Types of Prayer

Even though you can ask God for anything, the way in which you offer your prayers will vary according to what you are asking for. That's because there are different types of prayers, and getting your prayers answered involves first knowing what type of prayer you need to offer, and second, how God prefers to answer these prayers.

The two types of prayer are:

1. *Question-Type Prayers*
2. *Intervention-Type Prayers*

Prayer type # 1 – Asking God for Answers

When you ask God to answer your questions, give you insight into a particular issue, or grant you peace about something, you're offering a question-type prayer. Praying this way literally allows you to receive direction from God, someone who knows everything about everything. Let me tell you why that's so important.

Typically when you're looking to get information or answers to your questions, you have to decide if the source you're consulting is credible, or if that source actually knows anything worth knowing. However, with God, you never have to worry about that because He is all-knowing. When you ask Him something, you can be assured that His answer will be right. Plus, He will always do what is in your best interest. He will use His foresight to bless your life.

With that said, God can respond to your question-type prayers in one of three ways. First, He can answer these prayers directly. Second, He can answer them through someone else, and third, He can answer them through the Scriptures.

God Can Answer Prayers:

1. *Directly*
2. *Through Someone Else*
3. *Through the Scriptures*

1. Answering Your Prayers Directly

During the course of my interviews with people who pray, I was occasionally disappointed to learn that some of these people didn't know how God could talk to them or how God could answer their prayers. Particularly their question-type prayers. They just figured that prayer was a one-way conversation. Let me assure you that nothing could be further from the truth.

God Communicates Via the Holy Ghost

When you ask God questions, He does listen, and He can answer. But how exactly does He do this? In John 14:26, Jesus reveals the answer.

> *But the Helper, the Holy Spirit, whom the Father will send in my name, he will teach you all things and bring to your remembrance all that I have said to you.*

The Helper or the Holy Ghost is the means whereby God can communicate with you or "teach you all things." But how exactly does the Holy Ghost work?

While I can't speak for everyone, for me, the Holy Ghost works more like a feeling than an actual voice. This feeling can sometimes be subtle, and at other times, it can be very powerful. It is a sense of peace that completely envelops my body. A feeling of warmth and assurance that lets me know what I am thinking or sensing is right. It is very real and very tangible, and fills my mind with complete clarity. Indeed, the Holy Ghost, or God's Spirit, is a very powerful means whereby God communicates with me, and it can be for you, too.

I've Learned to Listen

I remember a time in college when I had run out of money for the week and had no food. One morning as I was going to class, I began to pray in my heart. I said, "Heavenly Father, I have no money. I don't know how I'm going to eat today, but I've been taught to pray and ask you for all things. So I'm asking you, please help me somehow find some food."

Then, as I made my way on campus, I had a distinct impression that I should go to this certain building, but I shrugged it off. I thought, "That's just a feeling." Then it came again. It even came a third time. So, instead of going to my class, I listened to the feeling and walked into the building. I couldn't believe my eyes. I saw a huge table of food that was in place for some kind of conference. As soon as I walked in, a lady said, "Oh, come in and make yourself a plate. Come and eat." I made a huge plate of food. It was such a testimony to me that God answers our prayers. Those feelings we have in our heart is God's way of talking to us.

Setema G. - Utah

The Fruit of the Spirit

To further highlight what the Holy Ghost can feel like, allow me to share a Scripture from Paul's letters to the Galatians.

> *But the fruit of the Spirit is love, joy, peace, patience, kindness, goodness, faithfulness.*
>
> (Galatians 5:22)

This beautiful passage perfectly describes what a manifestation from the Holy Ghost can feel like and gives insight into what you should be looking for when asking God to speak to you. Feelings of love, joy, and peace come from Heavenly Father, and they are given to help you know when He is trying to tell you something. To help you identify these feelings, try thinking of a time when you have felt the way that Paul described. Perhaps it's been as recent as reading some of the stories in this book.

If the answer you present before God is right, you will experience the clarity, peace, love, and joy that comes from the Holy Ghost.

Another description of what the Holy Ghost can feel like is found in the book of Luke. Here, we read of two of Jesus' disciples, who were traveling on the road to Emmaus. After the resurrected Jesus appeared to them, they described how they felt a burning within their hearts.

> *They said to each other, "Did not our hearts burn within us while he talked to us on the road, while he opened to us the Scriptures?"*
>
> (Luke 24:32)

With this in mind, the next time you ask God to give you answers to your questions, will you pay attention to your feelings? Look for what Paul talked about when he described the fruits of the Spirit, the feelings of love, joy, and peace. Try to identify the "burning within your heart" that the disciples on the road to Emmaus talked about. As you do this, know that these feelings come from God and they are His way of speaking to you via the Holy Ghost.

Praying the Right Way

I had been offered a new job on the other side of the country. Accepting this job would mean uprooting my wife and three kids from our home of over ten years. My concern wasn't so much about whether the job was a good fit for me. It was more about whether the job would be a good fit for my family. Having my kids adjust to new schools and meet new friends, that really weighed on my mind.

After looking at all of the pros and cons, I decided that taking the job was the right thing to do. But I wanted to see what God thought, so I took my decision to Him. My prayers involved my telling Him that I thought taking the job would be a good thing for my family. Then I asked Him if I were right. I guess you could say that I wanted God to look into the future, and either give me the green light to go, or warn me about potential hazards.

Even though I put a lot of effort into my prayers, I couldn't seem to get an answer about what to do. Finally, as I was praying one night, I realized that I wasn't praying the right way. I was telling God what I was going to do as opposed to asking Him if my decision was right. I wasn't allowing for the possibility that I could be wrong. I wasn't approaching God with an open mind and a willingness to accept whatever He had to say.

With this in mind, I asked God about my decision again. But, this time, I asked for His confirmation with the willingness to accept whatever He wanted me to do.

I said, "Heavenly Father, I have thought about this job, and I would like to take it. I know it will be difficult for my family, but, in the long run, I think we will be better off. Is taking this job the right thing for my family? Please allow me to feel the direction from your Spirit and confirm to me what I should do. I will accept whatever you tell me."

Then I stopped talking and started listening. It wasn't long after that I felt the peace that I had been looking for. I knew God was telling me that everything would work out. I knew that, if I took this job, my family would be fine.

I learned a very valuable lesson during this process.

God wants us to consult with Him, but, when we do, we need to be willing to accept His will. We can't just tell Him what we're going to do. Instead, we have to talk with Him and be willing to do what He wants.

David J. - New Mexico

How God Answers Prayer

In answering your questions, God typically isn't going to do all the work for you. As your loving Father, He recognizes that you need to grow and learn and, oftentimes, do some heavy lifting for yourself. So, when it comes to asking God a question, calling on Him for guidance, or anything else, it's best to start by thinking about all of your options and arriving at a possible answer.

In doing this, you can certainly ask God for guidance, and He will give it to you. However, once you arrive at your best potential conclusion, you can then ask God if you're on the right track. Assuming that you petition Him with sincerity and faith, there are three possible outcomes as to how God might help you feel the peace of His Spirit and confirm if what you're asking for is right.

If What You're Asking God is Right

If the answer you present before God is right (or something that

God wants you to do), He will confirm this by allowing you to experience the clarity, peace, and love associated with the feelings the Holy Ghost. These feelings may be like what many have described as a burning sensation in their hearts, or, "a burning within my soul." Once again, think of the disciples on the road to Emmaus. After walking with Christ they said, "Did not our hearts burn within us." When God speaks to you via His Holy Spirit, your mind will be clear and you will know that what you are praying about is right.

If What You're Asking God is Wrong

Contrarily, if God is answering you in the negative, you'll feel confused and unsure about things. You won't feel the peace and warmth that comes from the Holy Ghost. In fact, you'll tend to feel the opposite. When God's Spirit is absent, you'll feel a lack of peace and a lack of clarity. You'll feel confused. You can take this lack of clarity, or lack of peace, as evidence that what you're asking for isn't right. When this happens it probably means that you may need to come up with a different answer to present to God.

For example, even though I've just included a story from a person who needed God's insight on a career change, I'd like to include another one. This time though, the story is mine.

Recently, a friend who was looking to start a new business approached me and wanted me to join him in this endeavor. Although this was a good opportunity and I entertained it for many weeks, every time I talked to God about it, I felt confused and unclear about what to do. I couldn't seem to come to a peaceful resolution about what to do. I concluded that God was telling me that this opportunity wasn't right. I subsequently turned down the offer.

A few weeks later, another opportunity presented itself. When

I prayed about it, I received the peace and clarity concerning the matter that was previously absent. I concluded that these feelings were from my Heavenly Father and He was telling me that this new opportunity was the right one for me. So far, this decision has proved to be right.

If What You're Asking is Neither Right Nor Wrong

Finally, if you feel neither good nor bad about your decisions as you pray, that's usually God's way of letting you know that you can do what you want. That's because sometimes, you're not choosing between good and bad. You're simply choosing between two good things, and whatever choice you make will be fine with God.

However, in times when you neither feel good nor bad about your decision, you will want to make very sure that you're truly asking God for His input, as opposed to just telling Him what you're going to do. Also, ask yourself if you've given the process your best efforts.

For example, I sometimes approach God prematurely and expect Him to give me answers to things when I haven't done my part. In times like this, when I'm looking for direction and I neither feel good nor bad about my decisions, that very well could be God's way of saying, "Come back to me when you've put a little more thought into what you want. Then I'll let you know what I think."

Be Still and Know That I Am God

Upon graduation from a doctoral program, I had to determine a career path. I had earlier decided to become a university professor, which was my original motivation for entering graduate school. However, upon graduation,

I found a very competitive job market in academia. I was fortunate enough to have multiple offers to become a member of various faculties, but none of these offers came from universities that I had hoped to join. Moreover, I had some opportunities to take some well-paying jobs outside of academia. But these jobs were in cities that really didn't appeal to me as places to make my new home. Finally, some entrepreneurial opportunities in my hometown were also attractive and worthy of consideration.

Using newly acquired analytical skills to methodically go over the various offers and opportunities, I eventually arrived at a conclusion. But it didn't feel right to me. I solicited opinions from mentors, family, and friends. Then, after spending the better part of several days in thought, I arrived at a possible conclusion. But something was still missing. Frustrated, I took my decision (and frustration) to the Lord and asked Him to help me. I had hesitated to do this because I felt that God didn't necessarily care what I did for a living or where I did it. Nevertheless, for the next several days, the primary focus of my prayers was seeking an answer to my decision, all the while watching the clock tick down on some of the offers I had on the table. No answer seemed to come.

Days later, I found myself driving on a long road trip alone with my thoughts. I was away from everything else in my life for just a few short hours. Then the answer came to me through some very strong impressions. The choice that was best for me wasn't the most financially rewarding or what I thought was the most emotionally satisfying, but it was the best one for me at that time. Furthermore, I had the confidence to move forward.

Looking back, getting this answer involved me setting aside all the decision-making activities and just listening to what God had to tell me, something I had not really done. While I was asking the same question repeatedly, God had been patiently waiting for me to listen for the answer. Ever since this experience, one of my favorite Scriptures is "Be still, and know that I am God."

Steve F. - California

Learning to Hear God's Voice

Learning how to distinguish the feelings of the Holy Ghost, such as peace, comfort, love, joy, encouragement, and so on, can take time and practice. But don't give up if this initially seems difficult. I promise you that, as you persevere, you will get better at interpreting God's instructions as delivered by the Holy Ghost. With practice, you will perfect the process of identifying God's voice.

As you do this, here are some things to keep in mind:

- Come to God with a decision. This will show Him that you have done your part in the process.
- Ask with complete sincerity and unfailing faith that God will answer your prayer.
- Don't tell God what you're going to do. Ask Him if what you've decided is right.
- Be prepared to accept God's will.
- Pray in an environment that will allow you to hear the Holy Ghost.
- Ask God yes or no questions. These are easier to get answers to as they show God you've come up with a possible answer on your own. Also, questions of this type lend themselves to the do-I-feel-at-peace-or-do-I-feel-confused method of discovering God's will.

The Holy Ghost is a very real and very powerful means whereby God can comfort you, guide you, and answer your questions. It can bless your life with the peace and clarity that is so often needed in this troubling world.

I urge you to practice identifying what the Holy Ghost feels like so that God might be a bigger part of your life. I know that as I have done this, it has made all the difference.

> *Sometimes, you might feel impressed to do something, and that something might be God prompting you to help answer someone's prayer.*

2. *God Can Answer Your Prayers Through Others*

On occasion, God chooses to answer your prayers through someone else. In fact, while you may be praying for something, God may be preparing someone to give you what you need. Then, even though it may initially seem like a coincidence, the person God has been influencing does something on your behalf that ultimately answers your prayer. Let me tell you about a time when this happened to me.

When my second child was about five weeks from being born, my wife went into early labor. She was immediately put on bed rest and it looked like she would have to stay that way until our baby was born. Certainly, I was willing to do whatever was needed for the safety of both my wife and unborn child. But, because I didn't have any vacation time left for the year, I was worried about how I was going to help my wife stay in bed for five weeks, take care of our two-year-old son, and how I could still go to work.

Over the next few days, my prayers consisted of asking God to bless my wife and my family, and to help me figure out how I was going to take care of them, particularly my son. He was too much of an active kid to let my wife stay in bed all day while I went to work. I really needed help, and I pleaded with God for a solution.

I have to admit, my initial thinking was that God would answer my prayers by helping my wife return to full health and strength. But that's not what Heavenly Father had in mind. Instead, He had a much better solution.

While getting my son to sleep one night, I received a phone call from my mother who lives in Australia. After some initial pleasantries, she told me that, although she wasn't scheduled to visit for about another month, she had a feeling that coming sooner would be a good idea. Now, even though my mother and I are very close, for whatever reason, I hadn't told her about my wife's condition. She had no notion of our situation, and her idea of coming to visit sooner than planned was strictly her own.

I told my mom about what was going on. After she questioned why I hadn't told her sooner, she announced she'd be on our doorstep within the week. And she was!

During the next five weeks, my mother cared for my son and the rest of my family. Her being at my house allowed me to continue working and for my wife to remain on bed rest. And, as a side benefit, my mom got the chance to know her grandson in a way that only a caregiver can. She developed a bond with him that remains very special to this day. In fact, I believe she was just as grateful for the opportunity to serve us, as we were to have her.

Looking back, the way in which I thought my prayer was going to be answered turned out to be very different from the way God actually answered it. Like always, God knew what was best and His way of solving the problem was better than mine. While I was praying for help, God was inspiring someone else to give me that help. God was aware of my situation and started putting things together before I even approached Him. He knew that things were getting too tough for me to handle and stepped in right when I needed Him.

A GOOD SAMARITAN

As an alcoholic, my life was a mess. I was living on the streets and figured that I was either going to drink myself to death or spend the rest of my life as a homeless person. I couldn't see a way out, and I was desperate. Now even though I wasn't living my life in a way that God would have wanted me to, I still prayed regularly and asked for His help.

One night I met a man who changed my life. While sleeping in a park, this man approached me and took me to a local shelter. But that wasn't all he did. He also started taking me to some AA meetings, and helping me begin the process of getting sober. For months every morning, this man would pick me up at the shelter and take me to the meetings. He had been sober for over twenty years and knew what I was going through.

At first, kicking my addiction felt impossible, but I continued to pray and ask God to help me. There were so many times when I really wanted to drink, but my prayers helped me get through these times. As I prayed, I often felt God's presence. I believe He was letting me know that He would help me.

I eventually got a job and found a place to live. Pretty soon, I started feeling like my life was going in a direction that I wanted it to. For the first time in a long time, I felt a sense of hope about my life.

I've been sober now for over fifteen years. I am so thankful that God answered my prayers by sending me someone to help me. I couldn't have done it without this person, and I couldn't have done it without God.

Richard V. - Texas

When God answers your prayers through someone else, everyone benefits. So if you ever feel impressed to do something, do it! Act upon any inclinations you have. It very well could be God prompting you to help answer someone's prayer. Chances are, you'll be blessed for doing so.

3. God Can Answer Your Prayers Through the Scriptures

Have you ever heard the phrase, "We talk to God through prayer, and He answers us through the Scriptures"? From my experience, this is true! The Scriptures can provide very real answers to your prayers. But getting answers to your prayers by reading the Scriptures involves more than just treasure hunting for guidance. Not that it can't work that way, but there is a better way.

You have a more favorable chance of procuring answers to your prayers from the Scriptures if you're a regular reader of Scripture. Instead of searching or hunting for an answer, continue reading the way you normally do, and let God guide you. You'll be amazed at how the very thing you need help with, often happens to be the subject you're reading about at the time.

It works this way because God is intimately aware of your every need. He also authored the Scriptures. Because He is all-powerful and all-knowing, He can coordinate your needs with His words. Through the Scriptures, He can give you the comfort and answers you're looking for.

Understanding Forgiveness

I remember a person at my work with whom I had developed a close friendship but because of some monetary issues, we had a falling out. Many months after leaving this company, I found myself thinking about this person, wanting to restore our friendship. However, as I thought and prayed about the situation, I found myself getting frustrated about what had happened, and my desire to reach out to him weakened. As much as I tried to feel at peace about the situation, I just couldn't seem to move on.

A few days later, I was thinking about the situation when I came across a Scripture that changed my entire outlook. The Scripture was in the book of Matthew, and it reads, "Then Peter came up and said, 'Lord, how often will my brother sin against me, and I forgive him? As many as seven times?' Jesus said to him, 'I do not say to you seven times, but seventy times seven.'"

As soon as I read this Scripture, I knew what I had to do. I contacted this person, and our friendship was restored. Doing this allowed me to feel the peace I had been looking for.

Doug S. - Florida

Answers to your prayers can come directly from God, through other people, or through the Scriptures. However, regardless of how God chooses to answer your prayers, be assured that He is intimately aware of your every need and He listens and answers every prayer. But you must be ready to listen for His voice and be willing to accept His will. If you do this and live your life in such a way to hear God's voice, you'll certainly start hearing it more and more.

Prayer Type # 2 – Asking God to Intervene in Your Life

Even when you try your very best, you will sometimes fall short of accomplishing your goals and fulfilling your dreams. When this happens, don't be discouraged. One of the greatest things about involving God in your actions is that He can compliment your efforts and make things happen that otherwise wouldn't. He can take your best efforts and make them better, and with His help you can more readily accomplish your goals and dreams.

> *Intervention-type prayers are offered to ask God to make things happen that normally wouldn't.*

Getting God to bless your efforts involves offering an intervention-type prayer. When you ask God to do this, you're literally asking Him to bless you with something you just can't do yourself. It might involve asking Him for help financially, physically, emotionally, spiritually, or in some other way. It could be that you're in danger and need His immediate assistance. You may need help for someone other than yourself.

Whatever your situation, intervention-type prayers are offered so that God might use His infinite power to make things happen that normally wouldn't. Best of all, when you ask God to intervene in your life, you're allowed to ask Him to bless you with anything. That means you don't have to hold back on your requests. Allow Him to demonstrate His awesome power and help you achieve all that you could ever hope for.

I Love That about God

I used to travel one to two weeks every month for my job, but, after having a baby, I resigned from my job to spend more time with my family. Then an opportunity came up to speak at a convention in Atlanta. Although I was nervous about going, I figured that everything would be okay, so I decided to do it.

When I got to Atlanta, I had an anxiety attack. I can't explain why, but I was really nervous and was worried about my son at home. I was just a wreck. I guess I didn't know how bad I was until a security person came up to me at the baggage claim and said, "Are you okay? Ma'am, are you okay? Do you need help?"

I don't really remember what happened next but I somehow made it on a shuttle bus and to my hotel. Even now, it's still kind of a blur to me. I just don't remember anything.

When I got to my room, I kept saying, "I have to go home. I have to go home. I have to get back on a plane. I've got to call the airlines." I had all of these thoughts, and I really thought I needed to be home.

I knew I needed to calm down and the only thing I could think to do was to pray. I fell to my knees and started sobbing at the bed. I asked God to help me to feel better and help me to know what to do. I just poured out my soul on my knees.

Then, the more I talked aloud in this hotel room in Atlanta, the better I began to feel. All of a sudden, it was like a light shone in the room and the weight was immediately lifted from my shoulders. God was there with me, and I wasn't alone. He told me in my heart that everything was fine. I didn't need to go home. I was doing what I needed to do and everything was going to be okay.

I don't know why I had this anxiety attack, but when I needed God's help, it was instantaneous. Maybe my little problem could have been miniscule compared to what somebody else was going through, but God gave me the comfort I needed and treated my problem with the highest priority. I just love that about God.

Christine M. - Arizona

Prayer gives you the ability to accomplish much more than you could ever do on your own. Best of all, prayer is free! Having God bless you is yours for the taking, and that's exactly what Jesus said throughout his life.

Ask, and it will be given to you; seek, and you will find; knock, and it will be opened to you.

(Matt 7:7)

Now, keep in mind that having God bless your life with the things you're looking for is conditional on your following the rules of prayer. It's also conditional upon you having faith. Faith in Jesus, and faith in believing that your efforts will bring about a desired result. In the Scriptures, Jesus constantly emphasizes the importance of having this faith when you're looking to accomplish miracles. In Matthew 17:20 He says:

For truly, I say to you, if you have faith like a grain of mustard seed, you will say to this mountain, 'Move from here to there,' and it will move, and nothing will be impossible for you.

But what exactly is faith, and how do you get it? Well, that's what the next chapter is all about.

Key Principles to Remember

- The way in which you go about asking God to bless you will depend upon what you are asking for.
- Getting your prayers answered involves knowing what type of prayer you need to offer, and, how God prefers to answer these prayers.
- You can offer two types of prayer:
    1. Question-Type Prayers
    2. Intervention-Type Prayers
- God can answer question-type prayers directly, through someone else or through the Scriptures.
- God uses the Holy Ghost to communicate with you. The Holy Ghost is associated with feelings of love, joy, and peace. Many have described the Holy Ghost as a burning within their hearts.
- Even when you try your very best, you will sometimes fall short of accomplishing your goals. By offering an intervention-type prayer, you're asking God to intervene in your life and make things happen that otherwise wouldn't.

Chapter Seven

Faith and Works

Whether you think you can or you can't, you're right.

Henry Ford

Faith

There's a scene in the movie, *Star Wars: The Empire Strikes Back* that I just love. It's where Yoda is training Luke Skywalker about the ways of the Force. However things aren't going as smoothly as Yoda wants. Luke has a hard time appreciating what the Force is, and how powerful it can be. So, in order to help Luke understand, Yoda lifts Luke's X-Wing fighter ship out of a nearby swamp. Incredibly, Yoda does this with just the power of his mind. Upon seeing this amazing feat, Luke says to Yoda, "I don't believe it." To which Yoda responds, "That is why you fail."

The need for faith is essential in receiving God's blessings. But what is faith, and how do you get it?

With practice, anyone can increase his level of faith...Faith is like a muscle. With work, it grows stronger.

The definition I like the most for faith comes from the book of Hebrews.

> *Now faith is the substance of things hoped for, the evidence of things not seen.*
>
> (Hebrews 11:1)

Putting this definition into everyday terms suggests that faith is having a belief in something that you can't necessarily prove or don't know to be absolute. For example, many people throughout the world, including myself, have faith in Jesus Christ. We believe He is the Savior of the world, He atoned for our sins, and that through Him we can be saved. Now, although Christ has never personally visited me, this doesn't prevent me from believing with every part of my soul that He is real and He died so I might be saved. This is faith.

Faith can also include the belief that your efforts to make something happen will translate into something you want. For example, for me, writing this book has involved a considerable amount of work. I believe this work will pay off when this book helps the people who read it develop a more powerful relationship with God. Now, even though I believe this will happen, I don't know for sure. This is faith.

However, more than just being a belief in something or a hope that something will happen, faith serves as the foundation for every single action you take and every single thing you do.

For example, if you didn't think putting one foot in front of another would enable you to walk, going to work every day would result in your getting paid, or exercising would help you lose weight, would you? My guess is that you wouldn't. However, because you've previously witnessed the outcome of these actions, you have faith that doing them again will translate into similar results.

The point here is that the faith needed to walk, get paid from working, or lose weight from exercising is the exact same faith required to move mountains, change lives, heal the sick, be saved from your sins, receive blessings from God, and so on. The only difference is that you might not have witnessed these "big things" actually happen yet, so you might not believe they are possible. But I assure you that, with enough faith, they are. In fact, with enough faith, anything is possible.

But how do you take the faith you have now, and turn into the kind of faith that can move mountains? The following three suggestions will help.

1. *Decide What You Want and Write It Down*
2. *Think About Your Goals*
3. *Remember the Miracles of God*

Before we discuss these three principles, please note that faith isn't something you either have or don't. With practice, anyone can increase his level of faith. That's because faith is like a muscle. With work, it grows stronger and can get to a point where it becomes unshakable.

1. Decide What You Want and Write It Down

Unfortunately, all too many of us are too vague in our requests to get God's help. We say things in our prayers like, "God, please bless me" or "God, please give me strength." But bless you how? Give you strength to do what?

In order to make your prayers as effective as possible, you must decide exactly what you want. After all, how do you expect God to bless you with what you want when you don't know yourself? Granted, God is all-knowing, but He typically won't bless you with something until you figure out what that something is. He's not going to do all the work for you. You're going to need to put in some effort.

Writing down and justifying your goals, turns your wish list into a mission statement and increases your chances of getting what you want.

Dream Big and Be Specific

To begin figuring out exactly what you want God to help you with, I suggest you take some personal time to think about everything you want to accomplish in life. As you do this, keep in mind that this is your chance to entertain all of your wildest dreams. It's an opportunity to script the outcome of your life. So don't underestimate what's possible. Don't sell yourself short, and don't be vague. Instead, dream big, and be specific!

Once you've figured out exactly what you want, it's really important that you write it down. This will go a long way in helping you accomplish your goals, and will further demonstrate to God that you are serious about improving your life.

When you get to the point where you are ready to put pen to paper, try to be as detailed as possible. For example, if you're unhappy with your current financial state, instead of writing down, "I want more money," try to be more precise and even a little more persuasive. Begin by analyzing why you want something and write about your goals from that perspective. For example, in the situation of wanting more money, my experience suggests that most people don't want more money for money's sake. They want more money so they can have a greater degree of freedom. Taking this into consideration, your goal of wanting more money might more appropriately be expressed like this:

> *I want the freedom that comes with being financially secure. I am looking to increase my net worth to the point where I can either retire or pursue other goals. I don't ever want to worry or stress about money. I don't want to be dependent on other people for my own security or that of my family. I want to eliminate all of my debt. I want to have enough in reserves in case of an emergency. I want enough money to buy the kind of home that allows me to feel safe and secure, and I want to own this home free and clear. I want to be able to afford to send my children to the college of their choice. I want the ability to travel with my family and experience different cultures and customs. I want to help people by giving to charity and paying a generous tithing. Above all, I want the freedom that comes with money.*

Personally, I think this is a lot more persuasive than saying, "I want more money." In addition to being more to the point, writing out your goals in greater detail and justifying them with a purpose gives more meaning to what you're trying to do. It turns your wish list into a mission statement and absolutely increases your likelihood of getting what you want. Furthermore, it lets God know you're serious about achieving your goals and that you're not afraid to work for what you want.

Courage to Pursue My Dreams

In college, like many students, I seemed to be always broke. At one particular time, I was taking a business class and my teacher announced a business plan competition that my school was sponsoring. To enter, students would have to write a business plan for an original idea. The really good news was that the winner would receive $5,000. That seemed like a fortune to me.

Over the next few months, I wrote my business plan. This was extremely time-consuming and very difficult. However, in the process of putting this business plan together, I prayed extensively for the help I so desperately needed, and the inspiration I often so desperately lacked. As I did this, I felt the hand of God in my life like never before. Yes, the assignment was difficult, but I truly felt as though God was making me more capable than I actually was. I ended up winning the contest and was awarded a check for $5,000. But winning this money was just the beginning.

I was getting ready to graduate, and I had to decide what to do with my life. Should I get a job, or should I try my hand at entrepreneurship and see just how good my business plan really was? After praying at length about what to do, I felt good about starting my own business. My prayers gave me the courage to pursue my dreams.

Although it hasn't always been smooth sailing and I got off to a really bumpy start, five years later, I am still in business, and I am now doing rather well for myself. Along the way, I have adapted my business plan many times. I have made it a point to involve God in my decisions and always ask for His help. As I have done this, God has always delivered.

Chris P. - Washington

I can't overemphasize how important it is that you decide what you want and write it down. The more detailed, the better. As you do this, have a purpose in mind. Decide why your goals are important, and approach them from that perspective. It's really key that you don't skip over this step in looking for God's help to bless you.

2. *Think About Your Goals*

In 1902, James Allen published, *As a Man Thinketh*. He based this work on a Scripture found in Proverbs 23 that reads, "As a man thinketh in his heart, so he is." Now although debate exists as to the interpretation of this Scripture, James Allen took it as there being an absolute relationship between what we think and what we become. He begins his book with the following:

Mind is the Master power that moulds and makes,
And Man is Mind, and evermore he takes
The tool of Thought, and, shaping what he wills,
Brings forth a thousand joys, a thousand ills:—
He thinks in secret, and it comes to pass:
Environment is but his looking-glass.

I love this excerpt because I'm completely convinced there's a connection between what we think and what we accomplish. But this connection isn't something mystical or magical. Rather, it's a connection between thinking and then actually doing. You see, as you start thinking more about what you want, you typically start taking the steps that will help you accomplish your goals, and it's the doing, not so much the thinking, that makes something happen.

Your Thoughts Lead to Action

When you do think about your goals, you shouldn't do it from a purely daydreaming perspective. Rather, you should do it from a perspective of "How do I make my goals happen?" For example, if you're looking to get a better job, your thoughts shouldn't focus entirely on what a new job will entail and how wonderful life will be with it. Instead, your thoughts should include ideas on how you're actually going to get this job.

As you entertain these thoughts, remember to involve God in the process. You can do this by using your thoughts as informal prayers. Simply start thinking about what you want, and begin a running dialogue with God. Doing this not only allows you to bounce ideas off Him, but it also helps you develop a better relationship with Him. Then, with God's inspiration, you'll begin to feel which ideas that you've been contemplating are worth pursuing.

Plus, if you're constantly conversing with God in your mind about the goals you'd like to achieve, you'll be more likely to take the action needed to accomplish these goals. That's because if something is top of mind, it has a far better chance of getting done. Having a prayer in your heart (or talking with God in your mind and in your heart) is the perfect way to initiate action.

3. Remember the Miracles of God

When I was about twelve years old, my mother gave me a book to read that was a compilation of faith promoting stories. This book chronicled a number of events where people exercised faith, and something miraculous happened as a result. Now, while I don't remember the particulars of any of these stories, I certainly remember how reading this book made me feel, that with faith, anything was possible. In fact, throughout my teenage years, I found myself rereading this book when my faith needed boosting.

I share this with you, as one of the very best ways to increase your faith is to read stories that highlight the miracles of God. That's one of the reasons I've woven so many stories and anecdotes into this book. I want you to gain a glimpse of what's possible when you have faith, and I want to help strengthen your faith.

In addition to reading the stories of others, the Bible is filled with hundreds of stories that demonstrate the miracles of God. Think about the Gospels that highlight the miracles of Jesus. Reread where He healed the sick, fed the multitudes, and even raised Lazarus from the grave. In the Old Testament, consider where Abraham had the faith to sacrifice Isaac; Noah had faith to build the ark, and Moses had faith to part the Red Sea. All of these examples are instances where something miraculous happened because of faith.

With that said, as you familiarize yourself with the miracles of God, please don't ever think that God only blesses other people. You are just as eligible to receive His blessings as anyone, and as you follow the steps to increasing your faith, you will start experiencing more and more of God's amazing blessings.

Our Miracle

At only twenty-one weeks into our third pregnancy, things took a very unexpected turn. I had just put the kids to bed when I felt a warm sensation rush through me, and I began to leak fluid in large amounts. At first I wondered if I had lost control of my bladder (which sometimes happens in pregnancy), but then I realized that my water had broken. I called to my husband, and we rushed to the nearest hospital. Some tests were performed and before I knew it, I was being life-flighted to a different hospital that was better equipped to deal with my situation.

When we arrived at this new hospital, a team of medical professionals informed us that because my water had broken, the chances of our baby being born within the next two weeks was extremely high, but because she was only twenty-one weeks along, the chances of her surviving were extremely low. If she somehow did survive, she would most certainly have severe deformity and brain damage.

My husband and I determined then (and mostly because of our faith and knowledge in the power of prayer) that we could make it longer than the average two weeks. From that day forward, I was committed to getting this little unborn baby girl to a viable stage, twenty-four weeks. The nurses continued to tell me that it would probably only be a matter of days until I delivered.

The days went by slowly, but I miraculously hit the twenty-four week mark. Each day was such an accomplishment and blessing. I was so grateful for the chance to have made it this far, but my celebration was short lived. I felt like something was wrong and I was right. Within forty-five minutes of feeling this way, my baby was born. She weighed only one pound and eight ounces. She was not breathing when she was born, and needed to be resuscitated. She was then kept on a respirator machine to do all of her breathing. The doctors informed us that she was in critical condition and she had a very slim chance of survival.

We prepared ourselves for the worst, but continued to pray and hope for the best. The first time I saw her, I just cried and cried. She was so tiny, and you could see all her bones and veins. She was almost translucent. She had so many tubes hooked to her, and I couldn't even hold or touch her. She was in a plastic home, or what the nurses called a "womb with a view," where she would remain for a long time to come. I finally got to hold her for the first time when she was two weeks old. It seemed like forever. She was so tiny. I thought she would break. But it was important for her to hear my heart beat and feel my love.

We spent a total of one hundred and three days in the NICU, (Neonatal Intensive Care Unit). There were many times we were told my daughter wouldn't make it through the night because of infections she had contracted. She was very sick, and at one point had gone all the way down to only one pound and three ounces.

We were certain that my daughter would need brain surgery, heart surgery, and eye surgery because of how early she was born. It was truly miraculous that she did not have to have any of these procedures. Doctors and nurses were amazed and called her the "bionic baby," and "princess of the NICU."

My daughter is now a healthy, thriving five-year-old! She is the happiest little girl with an amazing disposition. She has had angels around her. I know because I have felt them. She is our angel, our miracle. She has a purpose in this life, and because of faith and prayers, she will be able to fulfill that purpose. She is a true miracle.

I am so grateful to friends, family, and co-workers who were a part of our lives during this time. We couldn't have done it without them, and we couldn't have done it without God and the power of prayer.

Carrie D. - Utah

In addition to following the steps I've outlined above, don't forget that you can also ask God to increase your faith. Your pleas should include asking for help to increase your faith with respect to the exact things you're looking for.

As you do this, God will bless you with a level of faith that is truly unshakable, and you will begin to believe that all of your actions will have a favorable outcome. Whether that's simply putting one foot in front of the other in order to walk or achieving your grandest and most ambitious goals. Either way, your faith will make it possible.

Works

Once you're clear on what you want, have written it down, and have asked God to help increase your faith, the process is truly underway. But it's not finished. In fact, in a sense, it's only just beginning. The work you've done so far is more preparatory in nature. Next, it's time to do the formal work that will make your goals a reality. Doing this involves developing an action item list, asking God to bless your efforts, and going to work.

1. *Developing an Action Item List*
2. *Asking God to Bless Your Efforts*
3. *Going to Work*

Please keep in mind that, even though the work part of things can be hard, don't be put off by this. It's not like you're going to the dentist to get a root canal. Instead, you're doing things that will allow God to bless your life and make it fantastic. Following these steps will allow you to reap the unimaginable blessings that only God can give you.

> *Your action item list will serve as the blueprint for making your dreams come true.*

1. Developing an Action Item List

For the most part, merely thinking about something isn't enough to actually make it happen. Typically, you have to go out and do the work to make your goals a reality. Therefore, your thoughts need to include steps on how you're going to accomplish your goals. To do this, you will need to develop a plan or a list of action items that will allow you to accomplish what you want.

Creating an action item list involves getting out your pen, and writing again. Here's what to do. Think about the goals you have set. Now think about what steps you can take to make your goals a reality. Then, as you did when you initially defined your goals, write them down. This will become your action item list, and it will serve as the blueprint for making your dreams come true.

For example, let's suppose one of your goals is to be a better spouse. Your action item list might include things like this:

- Compliment your spouse on their appearance at least once a week.
- Help them with the daily household chores.
- Bring them flowers or write them a thank- you note at least once a month.
- Make a point to listen more attentively to them.
- Reward them with a day to themselves every month. If you have children, encourage your wife to get away for the day, or your husband to go to a sporting event.
- Always speak about them in a positive light.
- Pray with them on a daily basis.
- Be the first to say sorry.
- Have a weekly date (no exceptions).
- Be honest with them.

Granted, this list isn't exhaustive, but it's certainly a start. If followed, it would definitely improve the relationship you have with your spouse. Plus, creating a list like this will allow your prayers to evolve and get better. Your prayers will go from asking God to bless you generally to asking Him to bless you specifically.

For example, in trying to improve your relationship with your spouse, instead of simply asking God to help you in a vague way by saying something like, "Please help my relationship with my spouse get better," you could talk to God about one of the items on your action item list. Such a prayer might sound like this:

> *Heavenly Father, please help my relationship with my spouse get better by allowing me to have the conviction to follow through with my action item list. One thing I want to start doing is complimenting my spouse on her appearance at least once a week. Help me remember to do this, and help me to have the faith that, when I do, my spouse will receive my words as intended, will be touched by it, and feel good because of it. Please help her associate these good feelings with me and, as a whole, allow our relationship to improve.*

Sounds better, right? And it certainly is a better way of approaching God to help you with respect to the things you want.

Taking Stock of My Life

I had been praying for a really long time for something important to happen, but for whatever reason, things weren't working out. This was really frustrating. I had been taught that prayer could help us achieve anything, and I thought I had enough faith to make my prayers work, but I guess I didn't.

Right around this time, I was at church, and I was feeling pretty sorry for myself. I was disappointed that I couldn't accomplish all of my goals, and I even began to question my faith. Then my pastor began talking about what it takes to get our prayers answered. I immediately perked up. I was eager to hear what he had to say and wondered if I'd be able to figure out why my prayers weren't working.

During the next thirty minutes or so, my pastor delivered one of the most inspiring sermons I had ever heard. He talked about the miracles that Jesus performed and how, with faith, you could ask God to do anything. He said that our ability to benefit from God's power comes through obedience to the commandments. If we're not doing what God wants, we can't expect Him to bless us. My pastor also emphasized how we needed to do our part, too. We can't expect God to do everything.

I needed to hear that. I needed to be reminded that God requires us to be obedient to His commandments before He can fully bless us. Although I wasn't the world's greatest sinner, I wasn't a saint either. Sure, I went to church and mostly did what was right, but I knew I could do better. After hearing that sermon that day, I resolved that I would try harder to follow all of God's commandments, and put more effort into accomplishing my goals.

Over the next few months, I took stock of my life and analyzed the areas where I was falling short. I wrote down all of my goals and the things I needed to work on. Admittedly, this was an eye-opening experience, and I quickly realized why my prayers weren't being answered. In truth, I was asking God to do things for me, and I wasn't doing anything for Him. I wasn't living the commandments, and I wasn't doing all I could to make my goals a reality.

I'm truly grateful to have been in church that day and for a pastor who was inspired to deliver a sermon that I needed to hear.

Peter M. - Arizona

Once you figure out what you want, take the time to create an action item list for each one of your goals. Be as specific as possible, and don't be afraid to develop this list during your prayers. I can't tell you how many times I've been praying and contemplating how I'm going to accomplish something when, all of a sudden, a thought comes into my mind that I know I must pursue. This has happened so many times that I actually keep a note pad beside my bed so that, while I'm praying, I can quickly write down the things that are revealed to me and then get back to my prayer.

2. *Asking God to Bless Your Efforts*

Many times, your action item list may not technically be enough to help you accomplish all of your goals. But that's the really great part about involving God in the whole process. Your shortcomings don't matter. Regardless of how inadequate your efforts are, so long as you do your very best, God can intervene and make up the difference. And that's the whole secret to understanding what prayer is all about. God cares less about the specifics of what you're doing to accomplish your goals and more about the fact that you're indeed doing something, and doing it to the best of your ability.

> *Asking God to bless you is about establishing a partnership with Him. As partners, you both have distinct roles and responsibilities.*

God Can Be the Difference

Having God intervene in your life and make things happen that normally wouldn't involves offering the intervention-type prayers that we talked about previously. These prayers will allow God to involve Himself in your life and bless you with whatever you need to make up the difference between what you do and what it takes to get something done. An intervention-type prayer could be as simple as this:

> *Heavenly Father, I want to achieve all of my goals, and I need your help to do it. I pray and ask that you might assist me. Please help me do better than I normally could and accomplish more than I am capable of doing by myself. I know you can do anything, and I pray you might intervene on my behalf and help me accomplish everything I'm looking to do. Help strengthen me, guide me, and comfort me. Please help make my efforts count for more than they normally would so I might be successful.*

God truly can be the difference between you getting what you want or you coming up empty. But, God's intervention efforts are directly correlated to your work efforts. He's not going to do all the work for you. You must do your part.

It's a Big Deal to God, too!

I really wanted to make the starting five of my high school basketball team, and I prayed every day throughout the season that this would happen. With this prayer, God really had His work cut out because I was, at best, a very average basketball player.

I really did my part by practicing more than I ever had, and praying even harder. Then, at the start of the last game of the season, my coach switched the lineup around and had me start the game. For that final game, I was one of the starting five.

I love that God listens to all of my prayers, even the ones that might not seem like that big of a deal. God knows what's a big deal to me, and He makes it a big deal to Him, too.

Cody D. - Florida

3. Going to Work

Your action item list doesn't mean anything until you actually follow through with it and complete the steps. Faith by itself many times just isn't enough and the Scriptures tell us this.

> *For as the body apart from the spirit is dead, so also faith apart from works is dead*
>
> (James 2:26)

In order to garner God's help in all you do, you need to do more than just believe. You are required to work. This means you must follow through with your action item list. Think about it like this. We mentioned previously that Noah had faith to build the ark. He had faith that what he was doing was right and he would be protected from the pending floods. But Noah's faith wouldn't have counted for anything if he didn't actually go ahead and build the ark. His faith alone wouldn't have saved him. But, with his best efforts and God's help, Noah was able to accomplish this monumental task.

In thinking about the things you'd like to accomplish, after you've come up with a detailed action item list, go ahead and follow through with your list. Do the actual work!

A Partnership With God

Asking God to bless you is about establishing a partnership with Him. As partners, you both have distinct roles and responsibilities. Your role in this partnership is to decide what you want, figure out how you're going to get it by creating an action item list, and then follow through with your list. God's role is to inspire you, comfort you, motivate you, protect you, bless you, and give to you. He will never cheat you, lie to you, or betray you. He is always looking out for your best interests and wants you to succeed. Best of all, He can use His infinite power to help you achieve all of your goals. I don't know about you, but, to me, God sounds like the most perfect partner anyone could ever have.

Allow me to finish this chapter with one of my favorite quotes on how prayer needs to be combined with work. It is attributed to Saint Augustine, and it reads,

> *Pray as though everything depended on God. Work as though everything depended on you.*

Key Principles to Remember

- There are three steps to help increase your faith:
  1. Decide what you want and write it down. Writing your goals in detail and justifying them with a purpose gives meaning to what you're doing.
  2. Think about what you want. There's a connection between what you think and what you accomplish. As you start thinking more about what you want, you typically start taking the steps that will help you accomplish your goals.
  3. Remember the miracles of God. Your faith will increase as you think about the many miracles that God has performed in both your life and the lives of others.

- Faith is always accompanied by work. These three work-steps will help you accomplish your goals:
  1. Develop an action-item list. Write down the exact steps you will take to achieve your goals.
  2. Ask for God's help. Develop a partnership with God. Provided you do your best, He will make up the difference between what you do, and what needs to be done.
  3. Go to work. Follow through with your action-item list. Do the work!

Chapter Eight

The Rules of Prayer

Seven days without prayer makes one weak.

Allen E. Vartlett

The Rules of Prayer

As you have surely noticed by now, I like to include examples in my writing that illustrate God's concern for His children. I guess that's why I often rely on the relationship I have with my children. I see the interaction I have with them, and it helps me understand who God is in terms of all His sons and daughters.

Many years ago, my son asked me if I would buy him a Harry Potter Lego set. Now, although this Lego set seemed really cool, it cost about $100, which I thought was too expensive. I was torn as to what to do. On one hand, I wanted my son to have this set, but, on the other, I didn't want to just give it to him. In the end, my wife and I decided to tell my son that, because the Lego set was so much money, he would need to help pay for at least half of it by doing chores around the house and helping us out as needed. He agreed to this, and we worked out a schedule whereby, after eight weeks, he would have earned enough money for half of the Lego set. But this was just part of the deal.

I also told him that, for us to come up with the remaining portion of the money, he needed to act and behave in a certain way. This behavior included the need to listen to his mother and myself in what we asked him to do, have a good attitude, and be generally more grateful for all that he had. He agreed to this as well.

Over the next couple months, my son was really diligent in doing his chores. He took pride in marking his daily chart on our refrigerator, and he really did his best to listen to us and be thankful for all that he had. There was a definite and noticeable difference in the way he acted during this time. He wasn't perfect, but it was obvious that he was really trying.

His mother and I were so impressed with his behavior and hard work that, when it came time to buy the Lego set, we did so without reservation. We knew he had earned and deserved it. Best of all, we noticed how this whole process allowed him to feel a great sense of satisfaction and pride in having worked for what he wanted and eventually received.

I share this with you because it highlights the way in which God can often bless His children. You see, my son didn't need a Harry Potter Lego set. He just wanted one. As his loving father, I wanted to help him, but only under certain conditions. I explained these conditions to him and he did his best to follow them. Because of this, he eventually ended up with exactly what he wanted.

In a like manner, God has established rules that govern your ability to receive the things that you want. But what exactly are these rules?

There are three simple (but crucial) qualities that God wants you to follow for Him to bless you. These qualities are what I refer to as the rules of prayer, and if you follow them to the best of your ability, God can open the very windows of heaven for your benefit. The rules of prayer are:

1. *HUMILITY*
2. *GRATITUDE*
3. *OBEDIENCE.*

God doesn't like arrogance or pride. He doesn't like it when people walk around thinking they're better than others or when His children don't recognize His hand in all things.

1. *HUMILITY*

Being a recipient to more of God's blessings begins with humility. But what exactly does humility (or being humble) mean, and how do you go about achieving this?

A humble person is unpretentious and modest. A humble person does not think he is better or more important than other people. He has a genuine love and respect for everyone, and he doesn't do things for the recognition. He recognizes his weaknesses and always acknowledges the contribution of others. A humble person never boasts about his individual strength. He doesn't relish in self-adoration or seek the praise of others. In essence, a humble person quietly goes about doing good deeds while never looking for any credit along the way. If you've ever met a truly humble person, it can be quite life-changing. At least, it was for me.

Learning Humility From Others

When I was a junior in college, I had the chance to serve as an officer in the student government program. One of my roles in this capacity involved setting up monthly luncheons with the university president and ten or so random students. The purpose of these luncheons was for the president to get to know the students a little better and to hear their thoughts and concerns on issues pertinent to them and the university.

The university president had an extremely impressive résumé. He was a lawyer by trade. He was wealthy, smart, and very successful. He was an excellent orator, and he had the distinction of having argued in front of the Supreme Court. He had even run more than a dozen marathons!

Even though this man had accomplished so much, when you shook his hand, you felt like you were the only person in the room. He gave you his full attention. With a single look, he made you feel his overwhelming sense of love and respect. He had the rare and amazing gift of making you feel incredible about yourself.

At these student luncheons, even though the president was always being praised for being so successful, he never, not for one second, thought he was better than anyone else. He never brought undue attention to himself or boasted about his accomplishments. His only concern was for the students and their needs. When asked about some of his life experiences, he always gave credit to others, particularly his family.

As I sat and listened to him over the course of several months, I got to know a man who was certainly remarkable, but, most of all, humble. Without question, he was one of the most humble people I had ever met. His example made me want to be better.

I share this story with you because learning to be humble often takes emulating the example of someone who is already humble. But why do you need to be humble in order for God to bless you? Simply put, God doesn't like arrogance or pride. He doesn't like it when people walk around thinking they're better than others, and He certainly doesn't like it when His children don't recognize His hand in all things by being boastful. Under no circumstance will God reward this kind of behavior. That's how important being humble is to Him. In fact, God may even suspend blessings that He was going to give you in order to help you become more humble.

A CHANGE OF HEART

I was in a bad mood, and I wanted everyone to know about it. I was shouting at my kids and my wife, and I was complaining about everything that seemed to be going wrong in my life. Finally, my wife ordered me out of the house and told me to come back when I had cooled down. I grabbed my car keys and drove off in a mad rage.

Getting out didn't help though because, while I was driving, I started yelling at the top of my lungs. I must have looked pretty silly, but I didn't care. I finally came to a red light and upon stopping, I witnessed something that changed everything.

Crossing the road was a little boy in a wheelchair. He didn't have any legs, and he couldn't have been more than about twelve years old. He was all by himself on this busy road, pushing himself around. As he went in front my car, he briefly looked at me and smiled. I immediately smiled back and gave him a little wave. My disposition immediately changed.

I was no longer mad. Instead, I was ashamed for having acted like such a jerk. Here was this little boy, who wasn't dealt a great deck, and he wasn't complaining. On the other hand, I had so many things in my life to be grateful for, and I was complaining.

I immediately drove home. After telling my family what I just witnessed, I begged them to forgive me. I then went up to my room, got on my knees, and asked God to forgive me, too.

Now, every time I start to get in a bad mood or think that my lot in life isn't so great, I think of that little boy, and it quickly reminds me of how very lucky I am. Without knowing it, that little boy humbled my heart that day, and he has continued to do so ever since.

Rick M. - Texas

The Greatest Example of Humility

Please don't think requiring you to be humble is God's way of repressing you. It's anything but. Instead, being humble allows you to be a better person and achieve greater things, and God knows this. Think about it. If you're humble, you'll be more likely to be a good influence on those around you, share more, love more, and, in general, make the world a better place.

Plus, in addition to helping you become a better person, being humble allows you to more readily accept God's will. You see, sometimes your requests to God simply might not be in your best interest or appropriate for you at the time of your asking. It's important to be humble enough to accept this.

Just think about when Jesus was suffering in the Garden of Gethsemane, pleading with God to ease His burdens and alleviate His pain. Even though Jesus wanted the agony to stop, He made it very clear that He would accept His Father's will.

> *And going a little farther he fell on his face and prayed, saying, "My Father, if it be possible, let this cup pass from me; nevertheless, not as I will, but as you will."*
>
> (Matt 26:39)

As much as Jesus didn't want to have to go through the pain of the impending crucifixion and pleaded with God to perhaps "figure out another way," He (Jesus) ended His prayer by saying, "not as I will, but as you will." He had the humility to accept His Father's will. In doing so, Jesus showed us exactly what it means to be humble. In fact, His example in Gethsemane is the greatest demonstration of humility to ever take place, and it teaches us that we must always trust in God and believe that His plan is best.

In your efforts to garner blessings from God, please do all you can to make your goals a reality, but always have the humility to trust in God and the faith to accept His will. Whatever your situation, God knows what is best for you. If you're humble enough to accept this, my experience is that you'll be rewarded with even more than you had initially asked for.

When you say thank you to God, He considers this an actual offering and, accordingly, looks to pay you back or give you something in return.

2. *GRATITUDE*

Let's suppose you worked with someone who was always taking credit for your ideas. Would you continue sharing your ideas with that person? Probably not. Instead, what if this person was always thanking you for your ideas and giving you credit for coming up with them? Wouldn't your attitude be different? Of course it would. Now think about it from God's perspective. How likely do you think God would be to continue to shower blessings on someone, if that someone never acknowledged God's hand in what they'd been given? It's not very likely at all.

The truth is, if you fail to recognize God's hand in what He has given you, He'll be less inclined to give you more. On the other hand, if you continually thank God for all that He has given you and constantly demonstrate gratitude, He will continue to bless you. This process is referred to as the "cycle of reciprocal blessings."

The Cycle of Reciprocal Blessings

The cycle of reciprocal blessings is a remarkable process that allows for a continual outpouring of blessings from God. Let me explain how it works. As you know, reciprocity means to pay back or exchange something of mutual benefit, and that's exactly what happens when you offer thanks to God. He rewards you back.

Think about it like this. Have you ever been in a situation where someone has extended a very heartfelt and sincere thank you? It makes you feel great. It allows you to forget about whatever it was that elicited the thanks, and it makes you want to do more for that person. It's the same with God. The more you thank Him, the more He will do for you. Best of all, there is no limit to this cycle of thanks and giving. It can become a never-ending process whereby, as long as you continue to sincerely thank God for all He gives you, He will continue to bless you.

What an amazing concept! By simply thanking God for all He gives you, you can experience a continuous outpouring from Him for the rest of your life. When you say thank you to God, He considers this an actual offering and, accordingly, looks to pay you back or give you something in return. And so the cycle continues. Who else but a loving, all-powerful God would ever do such a thing?

GIVING THANKS

A few years ago, my wife and I were in a difficult situation financially. There was the prospect of financial relief on the horizon, but it depended heavily on the goodness and actions of others. In looking at the two possible outcomes, I was left feeling enormously vulnerable. There was approximately a one-month window of opportunity when this specific financial relief could have possibly entered into our lives. I pleaded with God for help. Night after night, I prayed.

I had no idea whether my prayer would be answered (in the way I wanted), and I prepared for the reality that it might be answered in a way that was different from that which I desired. I prayed for approximately three-and-a-half weeks for virtually the same thing. All while trying to remember that to give gratitude throughout the process.

Finally, the day came when my prayers were answered in the way I wanted. My wife and I were tremendously blessed and I was enormously grateful and relieved. God, as always, provided for us. However, getting our prayers answered the way we wanted is only the first part of the story. The second part is what this experience really taught me.

I decided I would give gratitude to God for this specific blessing for the same three-and-a-half weeks after the blessing was received. I also decided I would use the same amount of energy in displaying the gratitude I used in my petitioning for the financial assistance. That exercise brought far more into my life than the money ever did. My relationship with God was eternally blessed and enhanced.

From my experience, I would give the following challenge to all. If you spend a month praying for something, whether you get what you asked for or not, give thanks for a commensurate amount of time after your prayer has been answered, even if the answer is different from what you wanted. I promise you that, if you do this, your relationship with God will improve in an infinite manner and your life will be blessed.

Brad G. - Minnesota

The cycle of reciprocal blessings begins when you simply demonstrate your gratitude to God for all He has given you. As you do this, God then reciprocates (or thanks you back,) by answering your prayers and giving you even more of His blessings. This cycle, where God will pour out His blessings, is one of the greatest acts of generosity you will ever have the potential to be involved in. Best of all, it's there for the taking and simply involves saying, "Thank you," to God.

The moment you stop acknowledging God for all that He does is the moment that He puts additional blessings on hold.

Praying Versus Complaining

One night, I was lying by my daughter, who was three years old at the time, watching her go to sleep. While doing this I started thinking about how crazy my life had become. I had two children, a mortgage, all kinds of bills, stress at work, and an abundance of pressures that seemed to be taking over my life. To say the least, I felt overwhelmed, and I was worried about how I was going to handle everything.

Once my little girl was asleep, I slid off her bed, got on my knees, and started to pray. I was fairly exhausted, so I just sort of slouched over the bed, rested my forehead in my hands and began praying. Even though I use the term "praying," I should more appropriately use the term "complaining." Instead of consulting God, I was telling Him how hard everything seemed to be. Granted, God loves it when we share our frustrations, but I was doing more than that. I was whining.

Midway through this prayer, my daughter moved a little. I lifted my face from my hands to look at her and right as I did, she giggled in her sleep. It was one of the most precious thing I had ever seen. Here was this beautiful little girl, whom God had entrusted to me, and she was giggling in her sleep. At that very moment, I felt an overwhelming sense of gratitude for what my Heavenly Father had blessed me with. Tears filled my eyes, and I spent the next several minutes just looking at my daughter and thinking how lucky I was to have her.

As I went back to my prayer, I thanked God so much for my daughter, and all of my blessings. I no longer felt like what I was going through was that big of a deal. If anything, I felt ashamed that I had neglected to recognize all that I had and how I had overlooked what God had done for me. Sure, life felt kind of crazy, but so what? I had been blessed with a beautiful family. How could things get any better?

What about you? When you pray do you find yourself talking with God, or do you find yourself complaining? If you're complaining, what you're doing is telling God you don't appreciate His blessings. The moment you stop acknowledging God for all that He does, is the moment He will put additional blessings on hold. Complaining prevents Him from blessing you with everything He wants to give you.

On the other hand, however, demonstrating gratitude to God allows Him to bless you even more. Plus, when you stop worrying about all the things that seem to consume your life and start being grateful for all that you have, it allows you to see things differently and approach your challenges from a much better perspective.

So, the next time you pray, will you take a little more time than you normally would and thank God for everything you have? If you do this, I promise that it will allow God to further bless you.

3. Obedience

The final rule, or principle, of prayer is obedience. If you remember from earlier, God's love for His children is unconditional. But the full extent of God's blessings are reserved for those who call out to Him and listen to what He says. But how do you do this? Well, it is as simple as being obedient to the commandments.

Jesus Himself was the perfect example of obedience. He not only demonstrated this repeatedly to His Heavenly Father, but also to His earthly mother and father, Mary and Joseph. A great example of this is found in Luke 2.

When Jesus was twelve years old, He accompanied Mary and Joseph to the Passover Festival in Jerusalem. After the festival was over, when the family headed home to Nazareth, Jesus stayed on in Jerusalem. But Mary and Joseph didn't know this, and they wouldn't know until three more days. Once they discovered that Jesus was missing, panicked, they went quickly back to Jerusalem.

> *And when his parents saw him, they were astonished. And his mother said to him, "Son, why have you treated us so? Behold, your father and I have been searching for you in great distress."*
>
> *And he said to them, "Why were you looking for me? Did you not know that I must be in my Father's house?"*
>
> *And they did not understand the saying that he spoke to them.*
>
> *And he went down with them and came to Nazareth and was submissive to them. And his mother treasured up all these things in her heart.*
>
> (Luke 2:48–51)

Think of the implications of this story and how Jesus is teaching us to be obedient through His own obedience. At twelve years old, with the intelligence to amaze His elders, He chooses to honor His mother and father. He obediently leaves the temple with them. He could have stayed and conducted more of His Father's business, but He didn't. He was obedient, and I believe this is even more amazing than His awesome intellect.

God is aware of everything you need and want. If you do what is right, He will answer your prayers.

Seeking the Kingdom Of God

To me, the idea that our Heavenly Father would reward His children based on their obedience to His commandments makes perfect sense. All I have to do is think about my relationship with my children to gain insight into why God will bless me if I'm obedient. When my children listen to me and do what is right, I usually find myself wanting to reward them and give them things, all because they did what I asked. Well, guess what? I believe it's the same with God. When you do what is right and follow His commandments, He wants to reward you, too. There are countless stories from the Bible that highlight this very point.

Think of when Jesus instructed a crippled man to "Rise, pick up your bed, and go home." This man, who suffered from a debilitating disease for thirty-eight years, simply had to do what he was told ("rise"), and Jesus miraculously healed him. Naaman was obedient to God and bathed in the Jordan River seven times in order to be cleansed of leprosy. What an obedient faith! Or you could look to Noah, who was obedient when God asked him to build an ark. Noah's obedience was monumentally rewarded.

The bottom line is that when you do what is right and obey God's commandments, God will bless you. Like Jesus says in Matthew 6:33,

> *But seek first the kingdom of God and his righteousness, and all these things will be added to you.*

But what exactly does "seeking the kingdom of God" mean, and why is this important?

"Seeking the kingdom of God and his righteousness" means being obedient to God's commandments. That's right, those things that Moses brought down from Mount Sinai.

The Ten Commandments

You shall have no other Gods before me
You shall not make for yourself a carved image
You shall not take the name of the Lord in vain
Remember the Sabbath day to keep it holy
Honor your father and your mother
You shall not murder
You shall not commit adultery
You shall not steal
You shall not bear false witness
You shall not covet

You might say, "Well, it's easy to follow the Ten Commandments." And perhaps it is. After all, you probably don't make a habit of murdering, worshipping idols, or committing adultery. But what about the other commandments? Do you keep the Sabbath day holy? Do you ever lie, cheat, or steal? Do you ever covet your neighbor's property or take God's name in vain? When all is said and done, are you following all of God's commandments, or just the ones that don't require too much effort? Plus, don't forget about the two greatest commandments that Jesus gave to the lawyer who was trying to trick Him. To love God with all of your heart and to love your fellow man.

> *And one of them, a lawyer, asked him a question to test him.*
>
> *"Teacher, which is the great commandment in the Law?"*
>
> *And he said to him, "You shall love the Lord your God with all your heart and with all your soul and with all your mind.*
>
> *This is the great and first commandment.*
>
> *And a second is like it: You shall love your neighbor as yourself.*
>
> *On these two commandments depend all the Law and the Prophets."*
>
> (Matt 22: 35-40)

In truth, some of God's commandments can be tough to follow, and we often justify this by suggesting that some of these commandments just aren't applicable anymore. But I don't think this is the case. I believe that God wants you to live by all of His commandments. You might even look at the commandments as God's action item list for His children to follow. They are His step-by-step instructions that will allow you to have a happy life. Because of this, you shouldn't look at being obedient as a bad thing or something that will restrict you.

Instead, following the commandments will make your life better and not just because it will allow you to be a better person. When you follow the commandments, God blesses you. As Jesus says in Matthew, He will give you "all these things." And isn't that why you're reading this book in the first place? Aren't you interested in making your life the absolute best it can be?

When we exercise our agency by following God's commandments, God acknowledges our obedience. . . If you choose to follow God, He will reward you.

The Gift of Agency

Perhaps on an even deeper level, it's important to be obedient to God's commandments because it demonstrates your willingness to subject your individual will to His. It shows God that, even though you have your agency, (the ability to choose for yourself), you choose to express this agency by obeying Him.

You see, God gave you the ability to do whatever you want. You can choose right or wrong or good or bad. It's completely up to you. For the most part, no one can force you to do anything you really don't want to do. You're the one who makes the decision as to how you're going to live your life. And that's the way God wants it to be. He wants you to make decisions for yourself because this is the only way you can grow and learn, and reach your full potential.

Now even though the gift of agency is essential for your well-being and growth, it comes with an enormous risk. You could choose to ignore the commandments and live a life contrary to the will of God. Doing this would certainly put your salvation at risk.

However, on the other hand, you could use your agency to do what is right. If you do, God will reward you for choosing to follow Him.

It's similar to the cycle of reciprocal blessings that we talked about with respect to gratitude. When we exercise our agency by following God's commandments, God acknowledges our obedience. In a sense, He thanks us for our willingness to follow Him and submit our will to Him. Best of all, when God thanks us, He does so in a big way. It's that simple. If you choose to follow God, He will reward you.

Being Worthy of God's Blessings

Always remember that, regardless of your actions, God loves you unconditionally. He always has, and He always will. But, if you want Him to bless you even more than He currently does, then you have to live your life in a way that is pleasing to Him. Let me give you a simple analogy that highlights this.

Pretend you are the founder and CEO of an enormously successful company that is worth billions of dollars. Also, pretend that one of the many aspirations you had when starting this business was to one day see your children work with you and eventually run your company. Finally, pretend that the time has come when your children are ready to start working with you and learning the business.

Now ask yourself, if this were you, what would you be willing to do to help your children succeed and run your business? What measures would you take to ensure they reach their full potential? My guess is that you would do everything you could to help them be as successful as possible. On the flip side, however, as a responsible CEO, you're not going to let your children run your company unless they can prove to you that they are worthy of the task.

My point here is that the way in which you might hand the reins of your company over to your children is similar to the way in which God blesses His children. Yes, God loves you, and He wants you to achieve as much as you possibly can, but blessing you to the fullest extent possible requires that you prove yourself worthy. This simply involves following God's commandments.

Also (and this is very important), keep in mind that, with God, it's not so much a matter of where you've been as where you're going. If you're not doing the most perfect job of following His commandments, don't use this as an excuse to continue to be disobedient. Instead, make the necessary changes in your life to get back on track and know that God really cares only about what you're going to do, not so much what you've already done. Therefore, if you need to do a better job of living the commandments, go ahead and do it. I promise you that, as you do, God will begin to bless your life in some truly remarkable ways. In fact, He'll be most inclined to do so.

Follow the rules of prayer. Be humble. Be grateful. Be obedient. God will take care of the rest.

A Final Thought: The Blessings of Tithing

Although not officially part of the rules of prayer, in order to garner more of God's blessings, you may want to consider paying a tithe or giving to a charity. In fact, in the final book of the Old Testament, the prophet Malachi talks about the need to give tithes and offerings to the Lord and outlines a remarkable promise.

> *Bring the full tithe into the storehouse, that there may be food in my house. And thereby put me to the test, says the Lord of hosts, if I will not open the windows of heaven for you and pour down for you a blessing until there is no more need.*
>
> (Malachi 3:10)

I don't know about you, but having God Himself say that He will pour out blessings upon you, so much so that you won't ever need more, sounds really exciting.

Therefore consider paying a tithe or giving to a cause that helps advance the work of God. Doing this will carry untold weight when it comes to having God bless you.

If you belong to a church and feel comfortable giving to it, then go ahead. Otherwise, find a worthy charity and give there, even if it's just volunteering your time. I promise you that whatever money or time you give will come back in multiples.

Key Principles to Remember

- God has established rules that govern your ability to receive blessings. If you follow these rules to the best of your ability, God will open the very windows of heaven for your benefit.

- The Rules to Prayer are:

    1. **Humility**- Whatever your situation, God knows what is best for you. If you're humble enough to accept this, you'll probably be rewarded with even more than you initially had hopes of receiving.
    2. **Gratitude**- By simply thanking God for all He gives you, you will experience a continuous outpouring from Him. When you say thank you to God, He considers this an actual offering and, accordingly, looks to pay you back or give you something in return. This is the Cycle of Reciprocal Blessings.
    3. **Obedience**- God gave you the ability to do whatever you want. You can choose right or wrong or good or bad. If you choose to be obedient though, God will reward you for doing so.

- The more you give to God, in the way of your time, talents and energy, the more He will give back to you.

CHAPTER NINE

UNANSWERED PRAYERS

I know God will not give me anything I can't handle.
I just wish that He didn't trust me so much.

Mother Teresa

God Really Does Know More Than You

When it comes to answering your prayers (calling for miracles, turning situations around, righting wrongs, or whatever else you might be praying for), there may be times when your requests to God aren't answered in the way you want. When this happens, it's important to keep in mind that God knows infinitely more than you do and all of His actions are based on His overwhelming love for you. Plus, don't ever forget that we just don't know what God knows. He is in the unique position of knowing everything, past, present, and future. He knows what's around the corner, and He will take future events into consideration when He answers your prayers, even when the answer is no. Please allow me to share a fun little story that illustrates this point.

A few years ago, I took my son, who was about seven years old at the time, to the Rose Bowl football game to watch the University of Southern California play the University of Michigan. As the game began, my son noticed an ice cream vendor coming our way. Upon seeing this, he immediately asked me to buy him an ice cream. However, because the game had just started, I wanted him to wait a little while. I told him that he could have some ice cream toward the end of the game.

As the fourth quarter began, he asked me again to buy him an ice cream. I responded by saying that, as soon as an ice cream vendor came back around, I'd happily do so. From that moment, my son kept one eye on the game and the other looking for an ice cream vendor.

By the middle of the quarter, my son was getting worried that he had missed his chance to get an ice cream. I tried to reassure him that a vendor would come by soon, but this was of little comfort. His understanding of the situation was based solely on what he could see, not so much on what I was telling him. He hadn't seen an ice cream vendor for some time and concluded that they had stopped coming around.

I, on the other hand, was confident that an ice cream vendor would eventually come by. I felt this way because I had been to enough sporting events to know that vendors tend to circle the same particular area and an ice cream vendor would eventually come our way. I tried explaining this to my son, but to no avail. He was convinced that he had missed his chance to get an ice cream.

As you can probably guess, a few minutes later, an ice cream vendor came by, and all was well. It was really fun to look at my son's face when he saw the vendor. It was a combination of relief and bewilderment. Although he didn't say it, I think he was wondering how I knew with such certainty that everything would work out.

Later that week, I was thinking about this situation and concluded that, in many ways, we are all kids waiting for the ice cream man to come back around. As I compared my son's experience at the game to my experiences with God, I realized that, because my son only knew a fraction of what I did, he had concerns. In a like manner, because I know only a fraction of what God knows, if I let it, this lack of knowledge can cause me concern, too.

However, if I continue to remind myself that God knows everything and that He is always looking out for my best interests, it can make things much easier. That is one of the most valuable lessons that you can ever learn. The fact that God knows exactly when the ice cream man will come back around, is very reassuring.

If you continue to trust in God and accept His will, you'll often find that, even when your prayers aren't answered the way you want, God answers them in the way you need.

God Knows What You Need

Never (and not for one second) is God taken by surprise. He is intimately aware of everything we do, and He has a plan for each and every one of us. When you ask God to bless you, you should do so with an understanding that He knows more than you do and He always has your best interests in mind. Remember, above anything else, God wants you to be happy. And while you may experience disappointment from time to time, if you continue to trust in God and accept His will, I assure you that you will be blessed. In fact, you'll often find that, even when your prayers aren't answered the way you want, God answers them in the way you need. Just keep in mind what happened to Job.

Maybe more than any other man, Job had reason to doubt that God was looking out for him. After all, Job lost his family, his wealth, and his land. He also suffered from terrible physical afflictions. Certainly, it would have been easy for Job to give up and forget about God. But Job didn't do that. Instead, he continued to worship God and have faith in Him. Because of this, Job was eventually rewarded with more blessings than he imagined. However, looking at how Job was blessed is only half the story.

The real story is the way Job chose to act, even though he didn't know what the future held. Now I know this sounds obvious, but you have to look at it from Job's perspective. He was going through some really difficult times and didn't know if further travails were about to beset him. Still, he never doubted God's love, or the fact that God had a plan for him. He simply kept doing what was right and worshipping God. And, sure enough, everything did turn out, and he lived a very happy and fruitful life.

Like Job, there is no doubt that, at some point, you will also go through difficult times. Everyone does. But how will you react when this happens? Will you be like Job and have faith in God's plan for you, or will you turn your back on God and go it alone? The choice is obviously yours, but I assure you that going through difficult times with God at your side is profoundly easier than the alternative.

Closer to Home

I really loved my job, and I was grateful for it. As a high school teacher, I knew that work was hard to come by, and I felt lucky to be employed. My only complaint was that it took me two hours each way to get to school, and this was taking a toll on me physically. But the school district I worked for knew of my situation and had promised me a transfer. Each day as I made the journey to and from school, I would have a constant prayer in my heart. "Please God, send me somewhere closer to home where I don't have to travel so much. I am grateful for my job, but please send me closer to home."

Confident that my prayers would be answered, the day of transfers arrived. I went to the office and casually asked one of the administrators, "So where am I off to?" No one answered. A little worried, I said, "It can't be that bad. Anywhere has to be closer than here." Finally, I looked at the paper and discovered I was going to a remote and isolated school approximately eight hundred miles away. What? I was in shock. I had been praying to get closer to home, not further away! How could God get it so wrong? This was not what I had asked for. God obviously hadn't heard me right.

As the new school year commenced, I took up my position in this school so far away from home, still wondering why my prayer had not been answered.

One afternoon, as I gazed out of my new apartment window, I watched some kids playing football. I then noticed how I could see my school from my living room. For whatever reason, I then calculated the time it took me to get to different places within the community. I estimated that, from my little home, I could be inside the school gates within one minute and sitting in my classroom within three minutes. Then it suddenly struck me. I sat there in shock as the tears welled in my eyes.

How could I have been so blind and get it so wrong? God didn't forget me. He didn't get it wrong. He answered my prayer and gave me what I had begged Him for. He sent me to a school close to home, my new home.

God gave me exactly what I asked for, and I ended up spending two years in this little community. As I look back, my memories of this place are priceless, and I wouldn't have traded the experience for anything. But more than the memories, I realized that God knows what is best for us. Even when we think He gets it wrong, He really gets it right.

Jane K. - Australia

Reasons for Unanswered Prayers

While you may not always understand why your prayers aren't being answered the way you want, you do need to accept that sometimes, that's how it works. Perhaps the thing you were petitioning God for wasn't right for you. Maybe because God can see the big picture, He may have something in store for you that's even more remarkable than what you had originally asked for. Whatever the reason, if you've been asking God for something and it hasn't happened yet, you might want to consider a few other things:

- Is your request inappropriate? Could it possibly end up causing you more suffering than you are experiencing right now?
- Will getting what you want prevent you from learning other important lessons?
- Is your timing off? Is it really the right juncture for you to have what you're asking for?
- Is your actual request something that will benefit you and/or others?
- Are you sure you are asking for the right thing?

- Are you asking for something selfish, something for your ego only?
- Do you have limited vision when it comes to this request? Are you looking only at the immediate repercussions, or can you look further down the road with God's eyes?
- Have you done your part? Remember, getting God to give involves working. Have you done the work?
- Are you following the rules of prayer?
- Have you been patient enough?
- Are you exercising enough faith?

When you start asking these hard questions about the requests you've laid on God's lap, you may recognize areas in which you are falling short. You may immediately understand why your prayers haven't been answered yet. However, if you're still having a difficult time with getting answers to your prayers, and you're at a complete loss as to why, ask yourself the following questions.

1. *Am I Asking The Right Way?*
2. *Is Something in My Life Holding Me Back?*
3. *Am I Taking Action?*

Trust in the fact that God knows more than you do and He is always looking out for your best interests.

1. *Are You Asking the Right Way?*

Sometimes, when my children ask me for things, instead of asking in a nice way, they ask in more of a demanding way. I can assure you that, when they do this, it rarely works out for them. However, when this does happen, I try to encourage them to ask in a nicer manner and that doing so will probably result in me giving them what they want.

Think about your prayers and requests to God. When you ask God to bless you, are you asking or, like my children sometimes, demanding? Do you ever say things like, "I've been praying for months now! When are you going to answer me?" or "God, you really need to do this for me!" Even worse, perhaps you might have issued God an ultimatum by saying something like, "God, if you don't give me what I want, I'll stop going to church," or "I'll be a better person once you give me what I want." Let me assure you that this is not the way to get God to bless you!

Instead, when you ask God to bless you, do so with the first rule of prayer in mind, humility. Being humble changes the way in which you approach God. It allows you to ask God for blessings with the understanding that He knows what is best for you and His answers might be different from what you want. Plus, being humble demonstrates to God that you are willing to accept His will and do whatever He asks.

Once again, think of Job. He accepted God's will. In turn, he was blessed beyond comprehension. Therefore, when you ask God to bless you, do so in humility. Trust in the fact that God knows more than you and He is always looking out for your best interests.

Heavenly Moments - Earthly Heartache

I was a young woman in November, 1975. The phone rang, and the voice at the other end asked if I knew where my parents were. Their flight plan had never been closed, and my parents had been missing for hours since the pilot called in a Mayday.

I suppose the reality of their apparent danger started to become clear when my husband suggested we pray together. I wasn't ready to pray. There was no need for prayer because they were fine. I was six months pregnant with an anticipated difficult delivery. My father was a surgeon and promised to be there. He had to be there. My mother had just celebrated her forty-ninth birthday, but she had many more to come.

I was told that my parents had been flying for approximately thirty minutes before their white Bonanza single-engine plane disappeared into the white, snow-filled mountains. The newspaper reported the following day that it was the worst storm in recorded history of the San Bernardino Mountains since the 1930s. It was a ferocious storm that came out of nowhere. According to the news reports, more than sixteen inches of snow fell that day, and wind drifts measured up to four feet of snow. The last they heard of the pilot was that he was experiencing severe turbulence and heavy downdrafts.

The next morning, the search began. My prayers began, "Please don't let anything bad happen to my parents. Don't let any harm befall them." Day one went by with no results. The sheriff's spokesman was certain the plane was down within a mile of the airport. He was hopeful to find survivors. He had a complete ground crew and seven aircraft searching.

Day two went by with no results. My prayers intensified, pleading with my Heavenly Father to protect and provide for my missing parents. The search and rescue intensified. Four-wheel drive vehicles were added. They crisscrossed a seven hundred-square mile area, but found no trace of the plane. The spokesman now feared they had crashed in the storm.

Day three passed. I kneeled, not knowing anymore what to say or how to say it. Anything I tried to express from my own understanding sounded trite and repetitive. At this moment, I realized my words must come from another place.

Day four included over two hundred and fifty men searching from Riverside County, San Diego County, San Dimas, Montrose, and Sierra Madre. There were planes, helicopters, many men on foot, more than seventy-five men on horseback, and a fleet of jeeps involved in the search.

Day five, six, and seven narrowed the search to the Holcomb Valley that was already searched over forty times, but was to be searched again. I was told they were no longer searching for a rescue, but to find the crash site.

I prayed and begged for God to take away my pain. It was more than I could handle. And I did feel a sweet peace knowing who was actually in control. As long as I focused on Him and shut out the constant news reports, I felt peace.

Day eight and nine brought no results. It was then I heard the sheriff on the evening news say they would stop the search on day ten. I found my prayers came from a depth of humility I didn't know I possessed. This was when I found the answer to where I knew my prayers must come from. I told my Heavenly Father, "Thy will, not mine, be done." I begged and pleaded that, regardless of the outcome, I needed two things in order for me to survive this pain. The first was that they would be found, and the second was that they would not have suffered. I prayed this prayer all the day long and into the night.

On day ten, they had given up the search. The search parties were all descending the mountain to meet at the command post, prepared to give up in defeat. It was then one of the searches found a tiny piece of a flight map. He continued in all directions and found little pieces of debris until eventually discovered parts of the plane. It was apparent they had died on impact.

When I received the information, I felt tremendous sadness, but a stronger and very real confirmation came to me that something tremendous had happened. My Heavenly Father did hear and answer my prayers. I knew it with a certainty I have never had about anything before. I felt a peace that could only come from knowing what my mother and father had always known. That Christ lives. He died so my parents might live again, and through the power of prayer I could have heavenly moments in the very face of earthly heartache.

Kathy E. - California

2. *Is Something in Your Life Holding You Back?*

Let's say you've been praying for something, and, to date, nothing has happened. Could it be that something in your life is holding you back? Is there a sin that you've committed that is preventing you from receiving all of God's blessings? You might be saying, "Oh, everybody is a sinner. We all sin every day." While that is true, I'm not talking about the everyday kinds of sins that we are sometimes are all guilty of, like offering an unkind remark, telling a white lie, or expressing an unwillingness to share. Yes, these are still sins and require your attention, but I'm talking about the big sins, the ones that can separate you from God or the people you love, like adultery, pornography, cheating, taking the name of the Lord in vain, anger, and so on.

This sounds harsh, and it's certainly not my intention to be preachy, but, the truth is, God isn't going to bless you to the fullest extent if you're not living in accordance with His principles. Remember, the third rule of prayer is obedience. Being obedient to all of God's commandments is necessary if you want Him to bless you. That's just the way it is.

We live in a world where we're used to getting everything we want at a moment's notice. However, when it comes to God, our time and His time can be two different things.

3. Are You Taking Action?

In my experience, I have found that, when people don't get what they want from God, it usually has less to do with God wanting something different for them, and more to do with them just not doing their part. God isn't going to bless you with something until you do everything possible to get it. He knows that working for what you want will help you be happy and allow you to reach your full potential. That's why your action item list is so important to develop and follow.

With respect to your goals, are you doing everything that's required on your end to make things happen? Really think about this, and ask yourself in complete honesty if you're doing your part. Have you created your action item list, and are you following it to the best of your ability? Are you taking action? If not, then you can't expect God's full blessings.

With that said though, there are times when, regardless of your efforts, God may have something else in mind for you. Whether it's the health of a loved one, something for yourself, or any other prayer, we sometimes don't get exactly what we want. However, as this happens, always remember that God not only knows what you're going through, but He also has a plan for you. If you ever find yourself in a situation where you're struggling to make sense of an unanswered prayer, please ask God to help you... to take away your pain, help you heal, or help you understand. I promise you that He will give you what you need. Above all, remember some of the final words of Christ when He asked God,

> *My Father, if it be possible, let this cup pass from me; nevertheless, not as I will, but as you will.*
>
> (Matt 26:39)

If Christ is willing to accept God's will, you should be, too.

God's Time Versus Man's Time

Sometimes when we pray, we want answers to our prayers immediately. We live in a world where we're used to getting everything we want at a moment's notice, and we simply don't like waiting. However, when it comes to God, our time and His time are two different things. Let me explain.

Some theologians suggest that each of God's days represents about one thousand years to us. They base this thinking on the Scripture in 2nd Peter 3:8.

> *But do not overlook this one fact, beloved, that with the Lord one day is as a thousand years, and a thousand years as one day.*

Personally, I don't know how long one of God's days is, and I'm not sure that anyone else does either, but I don't think that matters. However, if we use the one thousand-year reference for fun, we begin with the idea that one of God's days is equal to one thousand years of our time. This would mean that one of God's hours is equal to about forty years of our time, and one of God's minutes is equal to about nine months of our time.

- One of God's days = One thousand of our years
- One of God's hours = About forty of our years
- One of God's minutes = About nine of our months

Perhaps you're asking God to bless you and you're expecting it to happen quickly. On the other hand, God is responding by saying, "Just give me a minute, and I'll be right with you."

Are you prepared to wait for one of God's minutes?

Key Principles to Remember

- When it comes to answering your prayers there may be times when your requests to God aren't answered in the way you want. When this happens, it's important to keep in mind that God knows infinitely more than you do and all of His actions are based on His overwhelming love for you.
- If you continue to trust in God and accept His will, you'll often find that, even when your prayers aren't answered the way you want, God answers them in the way you need.
- If your prayers aren't being answered the way you want, consider these three things:

    1. **Are you asking the right way?**- Are you asking God to bless you, or are you demanding for His help?
    2. **Is something holding you back?**- Is there a sin that you've committed that is preventing you from receiving all of God's blessings?
    3. **Are you taking action?**- Sometimes when people don't get what they want from God, it usually has less to do with God wanting something different and more to do with them just not doing their part.

- Be patient for God's answers. Be humble to accept His will.

CHAPTER TEN

NEXT STEPS

Character is the ability to follow through on a resolution long after the emotion with which it was made has passed.

Brian Tracy

Putting It All Together

I have a confession to make. Perhaps you're guilty of this, too. Typically after I read a good self-help book, I often fail to follow through with all of the suggestions the book gives. You see, while I'm reading these types of books, I get excited about what the authors are saying, and I tend to make all kinds of mental promises of how I'm going to implement their recommendations. However, by the time I'm done reading, I tend to forget the details of what I've read and exactly what I was going to do.

I don't want this to happen to you with this book. Developing a better relationship with God is just too important. Therefore, to help you follow through with the necessary steps that will allow your relationship with God to be stronger and more intimate than you ever thought possible, this final chapter is structured as a reference to which you can turn whenever the need arises. While I'd love for you to read this book over and over again, I understand that you may sometimes just need a reminder of the major points. So, here they are:

Decide What You Want

Even though God knows everything about you, all of your strengths, and all your weaknesses, He's not going to tell you what you should do with the particulars of your life. Instead, He wants you to figure out the details for yourself, which is really just another way of saying, "You can determine how awesome your life will be."

To do this, start by deciding exactly what you want, and don't hold back. As we've said many times throughout the book, dream big because God wants you to have the best life you possibly can and He can make anything happen.

Then, once you have figured out what you want, you need to write it down. Now I know this can be mundane, and you may be tempted to skip doing it, but please don't because it's extremely important. Writing down your goals will help solidify your intentions and further encourage you to actually do the work necessary to accomplish them.

I can't emphasize it enough. Make the effort! Write down your goals and be specific. And don't worry if you're not the best writer. It's not like you're being graded. Your words are between you and God, and He cares only that you're putting in your best effort. Remember, having God bless you is about simply doing all that you can and letting God do the rest. That's the way it works.

Develop an Action Item List

Too often, many people think that all they have to do to get something from God is to simply ask for it. Even worse, they think their goals and wishes will magically come true without any effort on their part. Now, while this can happen, particularly for the intervention-type prayers that we talked about, for the most part, it doesn't work this way. Instead, God requires that you do your part and work for what you get. That's where your list of action items comes into play.

Simply put, your action item list is a list of things you're going to do in order to accomplish your goals. If you're looking for more money, figure out how you might be able to get it. If you're trying to establish a better relationship with your spouse, write down how you'll make this happen. Whatever it is that you want, you have to figure out what you're going to do to get it. After that, you simply need to follow through with your list and have the faith that God will take care of the rest.

Ask God for Help

As we've mentioned throughout the book, the effort you put forth in order to accomplish your goals may or may not be enough to actually make them happen. But that's the great thing about adding prayer to your efforts. With prayer, God can make up the difference.

Prayer is what allows God to intervene on your behalf. It enables you to accomplish things that you just can't do on your own, and it can bridge the gap between your shortcomings and your success. Above all, prayer allows you to communicate directly with God and develop a powerful and intimate relationship with Him. There is no doubt about it, prayer will help you more readily get what you want and will make your life better than it otherwise would be.

Best of all, prayer is available to everyone. By tapping into its overwhelming power, no matter who you are, you have the ability to receive incredible blessings from God. If you want more money, a better job, to be a better parent, to have deeper relationships, or solutions to a problem, you can get it with God's help. God answers prayer. If you ask Him to bless you, He will. So, go ahead and ask. You have nothing to lose and everything to gain!

Have Faith

So very much of what you eventually accomplish begins with believing in yourself and believing in God's ability and desire to help you. The relationship between having faith and actually getting what you want is very real. Keep in mind that faith isn't something you either have or don't. Faith is a deeply personal quality that is literally a gift from God. With practice, anyone can increase his level of faith. Faith is like a muscle. With work, it grows stronger and gets to a point where it becomes unshakable and undeniable. Faith will serve as the very framework for receiving God's blessings.

Follow the Rules of Prayer

Receiving blessings from God involves following the rules of prayer, being humble, grateful, and obedient. Doing this is paramount in showing God that you are not only worthy of His blessings, but you will also treasure and nurture these blessings. God wants to bless you, and He wants you to succeed. Provided you do what He says, He has promised to help you. In fact, rewarding you for doing what is right is how God works.

Be humble, be grateful, and be obedient. If you do these things and combine them with heartfelt prayer, I guarantee that God will bless your life.

Some Final Suggestions to Make Your Prayers More Effective

Begin Slowly

You've heard the old adage, "The longest journey in the world starts with the first step." The same goes for prayer, and God understands this. Think about it like this. Consider when a child is learning to walk. He doesn't just wake up one day and start walking all of a sudden. Instead, over a certain period of time, he gradually develops the skills necessary to walk. He starts with a crawl. Soon he progresses to standing, and he eventually takes his first step. Over time, this develops into another step and then another. Much like a child learning to walk, when you desire to get more comfortable with prayer, you should start slowly, building a strong foundation from which you can expand your efforts to develop a more perfect relationship with God.

Be Patient

Unfortunately, so much in this world is designed to satisfy our need for instant gratification. We decide that we want something and if we don't get it immediately, we either complain incessantly or simply abandon our initial desires. In contrast to this, God tends to reward those who, like Job, are patient. He blesses those who prove to Him that they are worthy of His blessings. If you are patient and continue to call upon God regardless of your situation, He will eventually bless you and do so in abundance. Just because God does not answer your prayer in your time does not mean He will not answer in His time.

Practice, Practice, Practice

If you're wondering how you are going to learn to pray so God will hear and answer your requests, rest assured, it's not as complicated as you may think. Learning to pray and getting completely comfortable with the process is like mastering any other skill in your life. It takes practice.

You may feel you are stumbling along, but as you persist, you will find yourself discovering the thoughts and words that will bring you closer and closer to God. And even if you pray now but you don't feel that you're being heard (and you're not getting what you're asking for), just keep going. It will pay off!

Ask for Help

As you know, having God bless you has a lot to do with asking God for help. Now as simple as that sounds, we often fail to do this. Even worse, during these times, God has His hand stretched out, begging us to take it, but we sometimes just don't bother doing this. Allow me to share a personal story that illustrates this point.

When I was growing up, one night, my parents were taking us to see a movie and have dinner in the city. I know that doesn't sound like a big deal, especially in today's society, but, to our family, it was a very big deal, and as children, we were very excited.

Our night began when we caught the train into the city. Upon pulling into Central Station, our family prepared to disembark. As the train doors opened, I saw one of the train conductors hold out his hand to help me onto the platform. This offended me. Sure, I was only about eight years old, but I was old enough to not need help. I refused the conductor's hand and promptly fell flat on my face. So much for being old enough to do things on my own.

I wonder if God ever feels like this train conductor, extending

His hand to try and help us, only to be rejected? Unfortunately, I think this happens more often than it should. As humans, we tend to let our pride get the best of us, and we miss out on opportunities that might otherwise have come our way.

God doesn't expect you to go it alone. He understands that getting to know Him through prayer can be sometimes difficult, but He continually offers His outstretched hand to help. All you have to do is reach out and take it. Doing so could very well prevent you from falling flat on your face.

Create the Ideal Prayer Atmosphere

We've already talked about the Scripture in Matthew that instructs you to pray in private. I hope by now that you've committed to do this. However, more than just praying where no one can see or hear you, it's important you establish the right kind of praying environment.

To effectively pray, you'll need to start by getting as relaxed and comfortable as possible. Sequester yourself from the pressures of life and the expectations of others. Once you've done this, you're ready to really converse with your Father.

Also, it's appropriate to pray on your knees. Because some prayers can take a while, sometimes I kneel on a pillow and rest up against my bed. However you decide to pray though, it's important to be respectful, but also comfortable.

Pray Aloud

If you have trouble concentrating during your prayers, you may want to pray aloud. In fact, I believe praying aloud has been essential in developing my personal relationship with God. Now, don't get me wrong. When I pray aloud, I'm not talking at normal conversation volume. Rather, I'm talking in a whisper, sometimes even just mouthing the words. Doing this allows me to concentrate more on what I am saying and gives more meaning to my prayers.

The Steps of Prayer

Finally, when you pray, consider structuring your prayer by following the steps of prayer. These are:

1. *Addressing God*
2. *Thanking God for all you have*
3. *Asking God for what you need*
4. *Closing your prayer*

1. Addressing God

To begin your prayers say something like "Dear God" or "Dear Heavenly Father" or even "Father." Use whatever feels comfortable, but don't refer to God in any kind of slang way by saying, "big guy" or "chief" or anything else disrespectful. After all, how would you like it if your children always referred to you as "big guy"? I'm guessing it might get old.

2. Thanking God for All You Have

After opening your prayer, you can thank God for all you have. Being thankful to God and approaching Him in gratitude is one of the rules of prayer, and it's critical to getting your prayers answered. Best of all, being grateful demonstrates that you're acknowledging God's hand in all things, and it can literally entice Him to do more for you. Plus, demonstrating gratitude allows you to approach your prayers, and your life, from a better perspective.

Your problems just won't seem as difficult, and things will seem a little easier.

3. Asking God to Bless You

This is the part of prayer where you can ask God to bless you and those you love. It's a chance to converse with God about all of your goals and dreams and ask for His help in achieving them. Remember, Jesus' words in Matthew 7:7.

> *Ask and it shall be given you; seek and ye shall find; knock and it shall be opened to you.*

So go ahead and ask God to bless your life. After all, as we mentioned previously, you miss 100 percent of the shots you don't take.

4. Closing Your Prayer

After you've gone through the three previous steps, it's time to close your prayer. This is like saying good-bye. While most Christians, including myself, prefer to close in the name of Jesus Christ, it goes beyond this. We believe that God answers our prayers because of our faith in Christ. Therefore it's important to close your prayer in the name of Jesus. This might sound something like, "I pray for these things in Jesus' name. Amen."

No matter how you pray, know that God cares most about the intent of your heart. You don't need to have the words of any particular prayers down pat. You don't have to be able to recite Scripture by memory. All you really need to do is speak to God from your heart. Of course, you should be reverent, but don't stop being yourself. God created you to be totally unique and He is waiting to hear your authentic voice, unblemished and unadulterated. Just you… just the way He loves you!

Thank you for coming on this wonderful journey with me. It is my hope and prayer that you have gained valuable information from this book and that your relationship with God will improve because of it.

Please allow me to conclude by sharing my testimony about God and prayer.

I know that God lives! I know He loves us and is aware of everything we do and think. He has a plan for each and every one of us and wants all of us to live with Him one day. Prayer is a divine tool that God gave us so that we might have a relationship with Him.

I know that God not only hears, but also answers prayers. With His help, I have been able to accomplish goals that I never thought I could. I have experienced blessings from God that are truly magnificent.

I pray you might experience this, too, and discover just how much you can achieve with God.

I promise it will be great.

HELP ME INSPIRE OTHERS TO PRAY

I believe one of the best ways to inspire others is by sharing our experiences. So if you've experienced the power of prayer in your life, I'd love to hear about it.

Please visit my blog at www.jarrodbentley.com and share your story.

Thanks again and may God bless you with all the success you're looking for. May He bless you with greatness.

8545483R0

Made in the USA
Charleston, SC
20 June 2011